MARCEL & ME

Also by Paulette Frankl

Lust for Justice:
The Radical Life & Law of J. Tony Serra

Marcel & Me

A Memoir of Love, Lust, and Illusion

PAULETTE FRANKL

LIGHTNING ROD PUBLICATIONS
Santa Fe, New Mexico

Marcel & Me, A Memoir of Love, Lust, and Illusion
by Paulette Frankl

Published 2014 by
Lightning Rod Publications
P.O. Box 22749
Santa Fe, New Mexico 87502

Book design: Janice St. Marie
Cover photo: Max Waldman
Cover design: Janice St. Marie
Photos of Marcel Marceau: Paulette Frankl
Photo of Paulette Frankl as young woman: Suz Cameron
Paulette Frankl in whiteface: Paul Schraub
Photo of Marcel Marceau with Paulette Frankl backstage: Peggy Heller
About the Author photo: Shari Kessler

ISBN 978-0-9915094-0-9 (softcover)
ISBN 978-0-9915095-1-6 (ebook)

Copyright © 2014 Paulette Frankl

All rights reserved. No part of this publication may be reproduced, stored in a retrieval system, or transmitted in any form or by any means, electronic, mechanical, recording or otherwise, without the prior written permission of Paulette Frankl.

Printed in the United States of America

*I dedicate this book
to the silent code of understanding
that unites us all.*

Contents

	Acknowledgements	*9*
	Introduction	*11*
CHAPTER 1	The Power of Illusion	13
CHAPTER 2	The Fallen Angel	19
CHAPTER 3	Nipped in the Bud	21
CHAPTER 4	The Summons	27
CHAPTER 5	A Force Beyond Words	35
CHAPTER 6	The Letter	37
CHAPTER 7	On Wings of Desire	45
CHAPTER 8	Chasing a Mime, Catching an Illusion	49
CHAPTER 9	All in a Day's Work	55
CHAPTER 10	Phoenix Rising	65
CHAPTER 11	A Taste of the Divine	75
CHAPTER 12	The Ravages of Silence	81
CHAPTER 13	Aftermath of the Storm	87
CHAPTER 14	Lessons in Silence	91
CHAPTER 15	The Counsel of Hindsight	95
CHAPTER 16	Booty Call	99
CHAPTER 17	Wake-Up Call	107
CHAPTER 18	Joining the Crowd	111
CHAPTER 19	Live the Death	115
CHAPTER 20	The Price to Pay	119
CHAPTER 21	Stillness, Essence, and Restraint	121
CHAPTER 22	Healing	127
CHAPTER 23	I Recall . . .	141
CHAPTER 24	80th Birthday	157
CHAPTER 25	Homage	161
CHAPTER 26	Beyond Mime, Beyond Time	167
	Postscript	*171*
	About the Author	*173*

Acknowledgements

Writing a book from the inside of the matter is like digging to China with a spoon. I could not have done this alone, and first and foremost I give thanks to Ann Yeomans, Archetypal therapist, for digging into the guts of the matter so that I could inhabit this experience anew. Ann, I couldn't have done it without you. My forever gratitude!

Of course thank you is too small a word for my incredible editor Deke Castleman whose magic touch takes what's good and makes it better. It's a miraculous thing to be in that kind of sync with someone. Deke, you are the best of myself.

Thank you to Mary and Andrew Neighbour for being my rock-in-need with everything: book, writing, photos, art, friendship. You're fantastic and I can't thank you enough.

Thank you Robin Michael Wagner for the title.

Thank you dear friend and poet par excellence James McGrath for pulling inspiration out of the air and slapping it on the page.

Thank you Nancy Fay for connecting the dots that led to Janice St. Marie and all the rest.

Thank you to my amazing graphic designer Janice St. Marie. It's a miracle to join forces with another visionary artist who understands.

Thank you great friend Helen McLeod. You're always there for me in just the right way.

Thank you dear soul sister, Klaudia Tataronis for all those incredible dinners that nurture the creative spirit and fuel the soul.

Thank you beloved Grace Swanson for your wisdoms, compassion, inspiration and input.

And right up there is a big auxiliary thank you to "Sweetie," my beloved cat and spirit guide, who inspires me every day by sitting beside me at the computer and placing her paw on my hand as I work the keyboard. Who really is to say where ideas originate? Perhaps she is the ghost writer who is channeling Marcel!

Finally, a big thank you to all the special people in my life who have contributed to this book in so many ways.

Thank you to my amazing family: Nicholas, Purea, Manu, Maya and Paul for always being a loving support for me.

And thank you Marcel Marceau for being such a revelation in my life!

Introduction

This book is a recollection of my thirty-six-year connection with Marcel Marceau as lover, friend, artist, and muse. It's the story of an enduring relationship between two highly creative people who were absolutely right together in some ways and absolutely wrong in others. At the heart of it was fantasy and illusion, which perhaps is at the heart of all relationships.

The frailty of reality and the strength of illusion caused our paths to cross, tested our bond, rendered us bare, conquered space, and outlasted time.

Considering that illusion played such a strong role in our interaction with one another and that we only saw each other for short interludes over long periods of time, it's amazing that we experienced so much of the ups and downs of relationship.

Yes, Marcel and I were lovers, and this book is sexually active. In writing it, I wanted it to be as honest as possible. I didn't hold back regarding the sexual aspect, though I took this stance of open transparency with great fear and trepidation, mainly because Marcel Marceau remains to this day, seven years after his death, one of the world's most beloved entertainers.

My purpose in sharing this kind of intimacy is it has a universal quality that is of value. Marcel's creative vision, art, and work were *always* about "everyman." Onstage he was unique, but in life he suffered the same extremes of hopes and shortcomings as anyone. It was precisely this dichotomy that humanized him.

Chapter 1
The Power of Illusion

We are together as before. The magnetism of his appeal draws me to him: his tenderness, his sensuality, the immense spaciousness of his presence. I feel his face next to mine, the warmth of his skin; he presses himself against me from behind. He presses himself into my fantasies. His lips touch my ear as he whispers, "Meet me at the edge of perception and illusion. Journey with me to the edge of time."

I accept his invitation with the courage of the innocent, the bold, and the fool-hearted. I am skydiving into him: into the timeless affinity of our togetherness. He collects me into his arms and I surrender myself to him as we fly above gathering storm clouds into a welcoming sky of resplendent suns. A knock on the door interrupts this flight of fancy. The scene shifts to the backstage of a theater. The glare of spotlights casts shadows of shapes onto surfaces. There are shadows of pulleys, ladders, and coils of ropes. There are shadows of people passing by. Their shadows rise and fall along the walls as they pass. Footsteps sound in the darkness. Mirrors reflect everything in multiple images.

He vanishes into this lively darkness. I open the door. There stands a lovely ingénue in her twenties wearing a full-length black coat with lace at the collar. An extravagance of long blond hair frames her face. Upon seeing me, she turns and leaves without a word.

I close the door but remain standing there, waiting for another knock. When it comes, I say, "He's busy."

She leaves again but returns later. This time, he receives her, eyeing her eagerly, like a piece of cake. "Take off your coat," he says

She slowly unbuttons it from top to bottom, then opens it like a curtain to reveal her luscious naked body. Such unmarred beauty is breathtaking! He slips his hand under the fabric onto her bare skin, causing the coat to fall to the floor. Her nakedness is reflected from all angles in the rows of mirrors.

She throws herself at him, kissing him urgently, professing her desire for him. He kisses her back, long and deep, pulling her into him. She doesn't know I'm there—so close, watching it all from the shadows. I sense their heat. I sense her thrill. It pains me to see them together; I feel the twist of a blade inside. The flame of abandon to desire that licked me a short time ago now becomes a spear of anguish driving ever deeper into me.

I reveal myself, standing there in my own emotional nakedness, with tears running down my face. She runs out crying. I feel her pain for it is my own. I too run out of his theater, into the fresh night air, to breathe deep the wholesome breath of life. On the entry wall outside the building are masks carved in stone with the tragi-comic expressions of laughter and sorrow. And now I am infused with these dualities: the anguish of sorrow endured in trade for the elations of the heart.

The ring of my telephone jars me awake. I sit bolt upright, my body still resonating with conflicting sensations.

Who the hell could be calling me at this hour?

I untangle myself from the heat of the sheets and leap out of bed, into the chill of early dawn, in a flurry of nightgown and determination to grab that phone by the throat and silence its insistent ringing.

"Hello!"

"My condolences—" The voice on the other end is familiar. "Condolences! About what?"

"I wanted to tell you before you heard it on the news. Marcel Marceau is dead!"

The impact of this news forced a rude awakening that hit deeper than sleep or reverie. It buckled my sense of equilibrium. Something inside me pinched tight, went rigid, and snapped. A vital part of myself shattered, leaving a void in the wholeness of my being. It marked an end to my decades of "if onlys" with Marcel. I blinked hard to get a grip on reality.

I was in my artist's casita. The clear desert light was pouring through my window. I was surrounded with pink geraniums and yellow chairs and green-and-white hand-painted tiles. My art was on every wall. Pages of my manuscript were on my desk. News of Marcel's death seemed to shatter the effect of all this beauty and creativity. I wondered, why does it hurt so deep? Was it because my relationship with Marcel and creativity were one and the same? I was his muse. He was my mentor. We were friends. We were lovers.

It's said that when a person dies, their life unfurls before their eyes. This was *his* death, but *my* life that was unfurling before me! Abruptly, all the sunshine and beauty in my small casita mocked the cruel reality of his death. A light had been turned off and I was cast into emotional darkness. Our spark had gone out. Our time had ended. There were no more "if onlys."

With Marcel, time was always my nemesis. Our togetherness was timeless, but I had always wanted more. Our brief interludes were mere hors d'oeuvres to the feast that was never served. My fantasy was that our time of true togetherness would surely come, would surely have its day in the sun after the last curtain call, after the end of the applause, after the last of the audience had filed out and the house lights were turned off on the last performance. We would meet again in the spaciousness of our being for whatever time was left; we would come to know each other anew, marveling at the wonders of each other, communing in many languages on many levels, traveling without the need to go anywhere, because these landscapes and those places were already within us. We would offer to each other the best of that which we had saved for last. Our nakedness would be a testament to all the circumstances that had brought us to this long-awaited time together. We would draw and paint, sup upon the nectar of memory, venture into the supernatural. We would dare to share that most private of vaults: our vulnerability. This would not be a rehearsed spectacle dependent on waves of applause from strangers, but an unfolding of places so deep and so real as to be totally private. We would join hands—hands no longer well-formed and taut with the newness of youth but that had held the weight of life in all its paradoxes, that had caressed the joys and clenched the despairs and wiped away the tears and applauded the triumphs and dared to begin anew. Our circuitry would ignite, as it always did; it would lead us past my great and enduring longing, past Marcel in whiteface, to our undecorated selves and the pure radiance of our togetherness.

Oh yes, I knew well the power of fantasy and illusion. It was my constant companion. It had always been a motivating force for me. I relied on it to turn my lights on, to keep my motor lubricated, to pitch me over the top of the mundane, to turn a bad reality into a good dream. Fantasy was at the core of my creativity. And illusion was at the core of Marcel.

Space warped and I time-traveled to our first encounter forty-three years distant. Marcel's face appeared before me, that amazing face at the moment we first met, forever etched in my mind. He was forty-nine. His dominant French nose gave me pause to fantasize the corresponding length of other body parts. His sensitive lips and piercing eyes burned me. My heartbeat intensified, leaving me flushed with expectation.

When I first experienced him onstage, I had the impression he was performing to me alone, in spite of my cheap seat in the crowded theater. It was that strong, how the projection of his energy touched me and broke me open in my most guarded parts. Surely, those hundreds of other people in the audience could not be experiencing the same reaction as I was—it would be illegal! Oh, the joy of genius! If he was having this effect on me in a public setting surrounded by an audience of hundreds, what would it be like one on one, just the two of us? This fantasy was almost too much to bear. It gripped me in the gut and pulled hard, eradicating all reason, sensibility, even my good upbringing and a lifetime of socially acceptable behavior. It emboldened me to do things I would have never otherwise done for no amount of imagining or pre-supposing ever equaled the excitement of being with him.

My pursuit of Marcel Marceau was like a dog chasing a truck. What did I expect to do if by chance I caught that truck? Perhaps I thought it would make me feel bigger, not so insignificant and small. Perhaps some of who he was would rub off and I would feel like a "somebody" too. I wanted him to want me; I wanted his acceptance, his validation, his adoration. I wanted this experience to be mutual, not just mine alone. I wanted to experience him wholly, inside and out. I wanted to experience his circuitry connecting with mine. I fancied it would be the Big Bang!

The connection and disconnection and reconnection of those fibers of wanting formed a journey into the very heart of longing and an emergence onto the path of selfhood.

I stared at my hands still holding the receiver, the hands that applauded Marcel in countless performances, that wrote letters to him, that sketched him and photographed him, that picked him up when life threw him down, that caressed him through all the changes and challenges that came our way. These hands were witness to our times together and our time apart. They reached for him and they pushed him away. They carved out a life without him, yet always found their way back to him. It was painful to imagine that they would never touch him again.

Chapter 2
The Fallen Angel

The house lights dimmed, reducing the excited chatter of the audience to a hushed murmur. A loud insistent knocking sound issuing from backstage overrode the remaining voices, as surely as a judge's gavel, commanding SILENCE! The theater was cast into total darkness—all-encompassing, dense, boundless, and breathing.

Suddenly, I could no longer see the hundreds of people around me. My senses came acutely alive, running a quick gamut from excitement to fear. What if one among us awaited this opportunity with treachery? A hissing sound issued from the direction of the stage: something large and heavy was being dragged across the proscenium. I concluded it was the curtain, slowly drawing open, thus removing the only remaining membrane between the audience and the stage—where anything could happen. We were contained in our seats in this vibrant darkness of all possibilities. We were both vulnerable and primed, fully alert and enlivened for the power of mime.

Thunder resonated throughout the theater; streaks of lightning appeared overhead. It seemed so real I was expecting to get drenched. Strains of heavenly music from Mozart's *Ave Verum Corpus* filled the echo between riotous thunderclaps.

Suddenly, as if being thrust down by the lightning, an angel dressed all in white, fell to earth with a loud THUNK, crash-landing with a broken wing. When the angel's feet made contact with Earth, I sensed the entire paradox of the human condition, with all its beauty and malevolence, permeate through the soles of his feet. The heavenly angel, now disoriented and shipwrecked, picked himself up, brushed himself off, and limped toward strains of music and gaiety issuing from a nearby honkytonk saloon.

Once inside the saloon, the angel's senses were assaulted by sounds and smells unlike anything in heaven. The angel hung up his wings on the coat rack and signaled the barkeep for a stiff drink. With a backward toss of his head and a swirl of bravado with his glass, he slugged down the drink, then ordered another. The alcohol went right to his head and his groin, an area of his body he didn't even realize existed.

Not wanting to appear an outsider and emboldened by the alcohol, the angel engaged in the activities of the saloon: smoking cigars that he lit with a quick slash of a match on the sole of his shoe; flirting with large breasted, ample-assed wenches dancing, twisting, and bending in provocative postures that captivated his imagination; gambling with aplomb and abandon; fist-fighting with drunken, thick-necked bullies in a macho display of manhood.

It all made his heavenly head swirl. He staggered to the edge of the room where he leaned his arm and the full weight of his body onto a railing, while the room and its occupants swirled around him.

In truth, except for the presence of Marcel Marceau, the stage was completely empty.

Chapter 3

Nipped in the Bud

To me, the Fallen Angel best represents the character of Marcel Marceau the man: an otherworldly being sent among us to mirror back with grace, humor, poignancy, and eloquence the polarities with which we live and suffer. The Fallen Angel was a lost soul, disoriented, trying to find his way, filled with hopes and disappointments, nonverbally portraying emotions common to people of all ages and cultures.

In tracing the fabric of this life, I envision Marcel Mangel as a small boy at the age of five, his mother's darling and a bit of a mama's boy, sensitive, inquisitive, artistic, and above all possessing a heightened awareness of life and the ability to understand and caricature what he perceived. Barely beyond toddlerhood, his gift was already evident.

I see him performing improvised skits on the sidewalk outside his house in Strasbourg to the delight of neighborhood children after school. These simple skits involved great heroes. Napoleon! Heroes always strike the imagination of children and perhaps he cast himself in that light. His mother looking on, out the window, filled with pride at her precocious and talented young son. I also envision Marcel's father, a kosher butcher by trade and a fan of the arts, holding his young son's hand as they walk together to the cinema to see his first Charlie Chaplin film. That film was a revelation for Marcel. It gave him a mentor, a trailblazer, and a sense of belonging into a small brotherhood of masters, whose creative art form was *silence*. Chaplin opened the door to the realm of highly stylized ideas and emotions. I envision Marcel suddenly realizing his path in life, knowing beyond a shadow of a doubt that he was born under a special star with a special gift, that it was his mission to follow his star to the highest level.

Socially speaking, Marcel was a late bloomer, twenty years old and still a virgin, reconciling a riot of testosterone and idealism. Oh, how ripe with promise was life! He had begun his studies in theater. His innate talent was immediately recognized. He'd had his first taste of the nectar of the lotus.

Then came the Nazis, rupturing his destiny with the profound wound of loss, incurred just as he was experiencing the bud of manhood. German troops marched into the cities of France, wreaking havoc, leaving dread and death in their wake. The Mangel family, like so many others, were given thirty minutes to pull together their belongings and appear at the train station, to be "resettled" in Limoges.

Fleeing fear became a part of Marcel's makeup. The deportation and subsequent death of his beloved father in Auschwitz cut him to his core. Marcel and his older brother Alain left their beloved mother in Limoges to flee to Paris, where they changed their name to Marceau to avoid discovery as Jews. Alain's name was already on the Gestapo's list. They narrowly dodged a bullet.

Both Marcel and Alain joined the French underground's forces in Paris. Marcel's survivor spirit emerged. He put his artistic eye to use to alter the papers of young Jewish children, then taught them the basic discipline of mime: silence. Next, he posed as a Boy Scout leader and marched groups of children out of France, away from the storm clouds of war, again and again, into the safety of Switzerland. I envision his daily bouts with fear and his growing focus on bravery.

After the liberation of Paris, he joined the French Army. Along the way, he learned English, and due to his command of the language, he became a liaison between the French and the Army of George Patton. His artistic ability and attention to detail made him a master at altering documents. The bonds he formed with Americans at this time ingrained in Marcel the feeling that America was his second home.

The war interrupted his training in theater and mime. At the same time, the horrors of war broke him open and gave him the depth of personal experience that in turn later packed the punch to his audience, which was so explosive. Fear of capture and death, the need for silence, a masked identity, and rebirth became the cornerstones of his life.

After the war, Marcel resumed his studies with the great masters of mime: Charles Dullin and Etienne Decroux. Decroux considered Marcel his star pupil. I envision this old master hunched, beaked, and eagle-eyed, imparting his no-nonsense techniques to his young student, passing on his master-of-mime torch to the commanding talent of his star student, even though Marcel's attitude about mime was often in direct opposition to Decroux's. Unlike Decroux, Marcel felt that mime needed humor in order to succeed as a modern art form. Decroux was of the opinion that humor cheapened it. Marcel went on to polish his technique by performing with the great mime Jean-Louis Barrault, best known for his lead role in the film, *Children of Paradise*.

Marcel's spirit of independence could not be contained within the confines of traditional mime. Launching out on his own, he formed his own company in Paris. There, in 1947 at age twenty-four, he created his alter-ego character, "Bip," inspired by the Dickens character Pip, the young protagonist of *Great Expectations* whose own grand expectations fell through every time. Pip started out as a pauper, rose in class to become a nobleman, only to end up penniless, yet now aware that clothes, proper English, and money do not a true gentleman make. Marcel crafted Bip to represent Everyman. His signature burlap top hat with a symbolic fluff of red tulle on a stem for a rose symbolized the innate nobility of the common man: tough, sensitive, resilient, unrefined but not uncultured, and especially full of hopes, dreams, and travails. After all that Marcel had survived in the war, he crafted Bip to be indomitable, dreaming large while suffering the vagaries of life. Like Chaplin's Tramp and Disney's Mickey Mouse, Bip was forged to be a survivor.

Together, Marcel Marceau and Bip stole the hearts of theater audiences the world over, making Marceau one of the most beloved performers of all time.

He was known as the world's greatest mime, that was a given, but when I knew him, I didn't realize the full scope of his influence.

He struck the audience right at the gut level, bypassing intellect and going straight to their shared humanity.

Before Marcel brought his show to New York, he asked himself, "America has *everything*. What can I give that it doesn't already have?" His answer? "Silence!"

In 1955 Marcel and Bip took America by storm. It was love at first sight. The theater-going public had never seen anything like what he did in spaces that otherwise relied on sets, costumes, language, and sound, or even other performers for their experience of entertainment.

Instead, Marcel's theater was devoid of everything but a richness of feeling and an abundance of emotion previously unimagined. The silent pantomimed skits, with their beginnings, middles, and ends, interwoven with humor and poignancy, demanded total audience attention. Audiences identified with the hope and bravado, longing and disappointment, love gone wrong and despair of loss and death. They could relate to the humor of not taking oneself seriously and the courage to brush oneself off, readjust to a new reality, and begin anew.

Every show sold out. He needed larger theaters to accommodate the demand of ever-larger audiences. His success was meteoric, with standing-room-only crowds from coast to coast and every big city in between.

Furthermore, though it couldn't be known at the time, his silent form of visceral expression was breaking ground for the cultural revolution of the 1960s. Mime spoke to all the lost souls of the '60s, trying to find themselves in the New Age. The perceived shallowness and artifice of the '50s had left them starved for something deep. This dissatisfaction forced a turning point that exploded into the drugs, radical politics, sexual freedom, and spiritual seeking for which the '60s are famous, and mime was adopted as a simple yet profound artistic style that packed small yet played big. It could be performed anywhere. After all, there were no physical sets, no elaborate costumes, no scripts, no music or sound of any kind, no other characters. It was just performers in whiteface transforming space and communication with hyper-expressive body language. Street mimes sprang up everywhere, especially in California.

The art of mime became a phenomenon in the '60s and '70s in America, a form of street theater for anyone to experience as spectator or participant. Thus, the fine art of mime became a street variety of mime associated with the theater of life at a time when masses of the people—mostly under the age of twenty-five—were leaving home, dropping out of school, and searching for a new identity, a belonging, and a sense of self-fulfillment. Many people were homeless. Mime spoke to that emptiness they felt by giving them the language of the heart.

My first experience with mime was on a street in San Francisco while walking with a friend. A mime in whiteface came along and got into step with us. At first, I objected to this intrusion on our privacy, but the mime simply mirrored my objection. Then a crowd gathered. I felt embarrassed that people were watching, and I didn't want to be the center of attention. I was annoyed and afraid of exposure. He picked right up on my feelings and mirrored every one, my facial expressions, my shyness, my withholding, my negative attitude. I felt stripped in a public burlesque of myself.

Undaunted, he struck up a blatant flirtation that aroused my response of steadfast rejection, followed by his hurt, pouting, anger, and sadness. Finally, I smiled, which elicited a flicker of hope from him; he made a symbol of a throbbing heart with his fingers. Finally, a big grin sent him spinning in circles of joy, whereupon, just as quickly, the mime was gone, on to the next passerby.

Now, I was elated! It felt as though I had been pulled through my blockage of resistance, withholding acceptance for fear of failure. Better yet, I wanted to do it for other people. I thought, "I can do this!" In no time at all, I too was in whiteface and a little costume, working the streets as a mime. Of course, what I was doing bore no resemblance to the years of rigorous dedication, discipline, and training that Marcel logged in, but it deepened my appreciation for

Paulette Frankl, 1981
PHOTO: PAUL SCHRAUB

the power of body language and emboldened me to interact with the public in ways that were otherwise unthinkable. And it brought good pocket money.

Marcel always disdained the fact that the infinitely complex discipline of mime suddenly became a generic form of entertainment and income. It was too easy. But in a sense, it was all because of him. He had released from the bottle, and now it had expanded and could not be contained.

Chapter 4
The Summons

The '20s had *The Great Gatsby,* flappers, the Charleston, the automobile, the telephone, Art Deco, and the stock market crash; it also had the Great Depression. The '30s had World War II, Hitler, the Holocaust, Charlie Chaplin, Seabiscuit and the machine age . The '40s had the atomic bomb, the end of the War, the resurgence of business and ticky-tack houses: the commonizing of America to one-size-fits-all. The '50s had TV, Hollywood, Marilyn, Mickey Mouse, Marcel Marceau, and the bloom of mime in America.

The "V" for victory sign from WW II morphed into the peace sign of the '60s. The '60s had America's tragic war in Vietnam, the Cuban Missile Crisis, the assassination of President John F. Kennedy, as well as the assassinations of Bobby Kennedy, Martin Luther King, and other great civil rights leaders, the Beatles music, the seeking of higher awareness through drugs, prophetic wisdoms issuing from the mouths of twenty-year-olds, incredible violence at odds with the vision of a peaceful world. Jesus look-alikes were everywhere, madonnas with child at the breast danced in the streets, the civil rights movement was rampant; there was women's liberation, velvets and nudity, breaking all the rules, Woodstock, and merciless government crackdowns. It was a collision of the forces of dark and the light. It was a culmination of the worst and the best.

I was a wife, mother, and photojournalist in Munich when the New Age wave crashed ashore in Europe in the late 1960s. I was swept away by the force of its clarion call. This was more than a fad or even a movement. It was a new paradigm!

Starting in 1969, I stepped off life's carousel of painted ponies bobbing up and down on poles in rhythm to tunes of social acceptability to join the multitudes of hippies exploring new dimensions. I was responding to the summons of a higher calling.

We were probing levels of consciousness that were uncharted in the West and looking East, to India and China, for the charts. We went back to basics, to nature. We engaged in "losing our minds to come to our senses"—a phrase coined by Gestalt therapy guru Fritz Perles. It was a time of idealism, communes, and the notion that we all belong to the family of man. It was a time of struggles and breakthroughs; I waded into the tide to surf this rising wave, along with a whole generation of others.

For me, emancipation meant freedom of the feminine from centuries of patriarchal domination. It meant equality in value both in relationships and in the workplace. In 1969, I left our nine-year-old son with my husband, after eleven years of a marriage that had an appealing façade but an abusive core. It was a marriage in which I kept having a recurring dream of being hacked to death with a dull axe.

Out with the bathwater went a racy lifestyle, nearly five years of living abroad and a promising career as a photojournalist in Munich. I returned to my native California to experience and chronicle firsthand this New Age movement sweeping the country, presenting a new view of life through the lens of idealism, peace, and harmony. Social, political, and spiritual leaders appeared everywhere, and were just as quickly eradicated. I was inspired by the vision of the Beatles, Peter Max, Bob Dylan, Leonard Cohen, and the image of a young hippie girl who took flowers from her hair and placed them into the barrels of the guns of a police squad, proclaiming "Flower Power!"

I was on assignment from a magazine in Europe to cover the Free U—a New Age learning center without walls that taught getting in touch with one's inner authentic self and nature, freedom of expression, and freedom from physical inhibitions. Lots of nakedness, massage, candle making, crafts, and psychodrama were woven into the mix. At one commune I was visiting, a blond, barefoot bare-chested, long-haired Jesus look-alike wearing a beaded necklace and overalls with holes at the knees and a heart on the ass approached me with his open hand, bearing a bright pink capsule. "Here, take this. It'll do you good," he said with velvet eyes and the benign tone of a priest offering a sacrament. I didn't need to be told it was a psychedelic. I reached for the capsule and downed it before my rational mind could grab hold of or question my sanity, for who could refuse Jesus bearing an offering of consciousness in a pink capsule?

The ground distanced itself below me. I had the overview and at the same time the inner view. Words became sounds, intonations; meanings were measured by motivations, energy became visible in paisley patterns—frequencies that attracted or repelled. An indescribable peace permeated me. I experienced the interconnectedness of all things.

The parade of life danced itself out before me in fragments: women in full wine-colored velvet skirts. Tiers of silver earrings. Long curly hair. Chains of beaded necklaces. A ring on every finger. Patchwork clothing. Tall boots. Bare feet. Bare breasts. Babies, dogs, goats. Trays of trinketry, some things of value, some just broken tokens of beauty: crystals, feathers, buttons, bits. Dancing to the music of the spheres. Crowds of people mingling, fingering things, touching one another; many trays, many fingers. A hand touches and admires; when it's done, half of the contents are missing; they reappear somewhere else, while more things vanish in the dance of quick fingers, so deft, so part of the display of life where everything is a gain and a loss. Magic is afoot everywhere—the magician's touch bringing everything to life, as a spectacle in Maya's Grand Palace of Illusion. People have, take, give, trade, the river of desire and fear, one minute a want, the next a caress, the next a loss, a new attachment, a new separation.

Eros, too, is everywhere: in the full lips and undulating hips of a young girl; in the graceful twist of a wrist; in the lips of a baby suckling a naked breast, in the leaves that touch and quiver, in the caress of clouds merging into one and pulling apart to allow passage of a pool of light. I know the moves, I've been had; I see my wares in someone else's hands. It's all a river, a flow of take and taken, the gypsy reads your palm while picking your pocket; the lover promises tomorrow while stealing today. Great talent, great longing, great cunning, desires met, there's always more to have, to lose, to want! Oh, the wanting! I'm no longer who I was: that too has been taken to make way for who I want to become, but I'm not quite there yet. I'm somewhere between in this scene. The banquet is half over and not yet begun; it's colorful, graceful, and fast moving, but not rushed. Nothing matters because it's all in flux; time is a part of the more and the less. I've never felt so alive!

I tuned in and turned on. By summer's end there was no turning back. I returned to Munich and my husband just long enough to pack my things and bid adieu to the life I had known. My soul's pilgrimage was being called forth.

This uprooting was radical in every way. It transplanted me from the comforts of urban life—job, family, friends, great cuisine, infidelities— to that of a waif out of my comfort zone in every way but the conviction that I was on the right path. I didn't even understand the language these hippies were speaking in my own native California. I was not a pot head; I wasn't cool, groovy or hip. Instead, I was square. This thing of losing your mind and coming to your senses came at a high price of letting go.

I hooked up with a beautiful young hippie man ten years my junior, whom I barely knew, and moved onto a seventy-four-acre abandoned apple farm high in the Santa Cruz mountains of central California. Dennis was savvy about how to live on the land. He had been instrumental in starting a successful commune in Oregon. My husband and I had purchased the land when we first married, but we never homesteaded it. It was now eleven years later and I needed a place to live.

One afternoon, as Dennis and I were lying naked in the sunshine, smoking a joint amid the blooming apple trees, Dennis said, "I'm moving onto this land. You can move into a hotel if you want." That's the way it was in those days. Ownership was a state of mind.

I replied, "I'll join you."

And so began my twenty-one years on Good Day Farm.

The farm was situated an arm's length from the intersection of three major fault lines: the San Andreas, the Loma Prieta, and the Green Valley faults. It gave the place an uncanny intensity, sometimes peaceful, sometimes destructive, always portentous.

We were definitely starting from zero. Everything about the place was a wreck. Where and how to begin? Our life of back to basics, back to nature, was built one step, one board, one day at a time. It was a time of sheer grit, great closeness, soulful fulfillment, horrible fights, difficult adaptation, and raw determination. I bathed with the garden hose for the first year. When it snowed, that water was real cold. The small potbelly stove in the un-insulated, sixteen-by-sixteen foot, hundred-year-old redwood cabin was the only source of heat; it had to be rekindled all night long. The toilet consisted of acres of open land and a shovel. There was also no lock on the door, and the closest neighbor was a half a mile away. We shared the cabin with its squatters: bats, snakes, mice, and a wall of active bee hives. My first back-to-nature lesson was to get over the urge to kill.

As there was no form of external entertainment, we made music at night with pots and pans, anything we could tap for rhythm. We read aloud to each other. Creating simple meals from what we grew was both delicious and soul-satisfying. I learned basic animal husbandry to tend to the many mishaps that befell the numerous animals in our fold. I learned gardening and pruning and composting and, most of all, the language of animals, plants, and the earth. In a kind of reflection of America's wars in Vietnam, Cambodia, and elsewhere, we were robbed six times in the first eleven months. I learned the truth in the Dalai Lama's wisdom that there is only as much peace as there are peaceful people.

In addition, ridding ourselves of the enemies within was an ongoing challenge. My relationship with Dennis only survived a couple of years, but I continued to live this lifestyle for the next twenty-one years. Sometimes my son Nicholas stayed with me, sometimes a boyfriend, but most of that time, I lived alone, just me and the animals in the all-encompassing presence of nature. I liked it to the degree that I liked myself. It was glorious in some ways, always challenging, mostly peaceful, and agonizing when I fell apart at the seams from abject loneliness and feelings of inadequacy.

Years later, close friends and my ex-husband bought the adjoining properties, and for a while we enjoyed a sense of community until the shit hit the fan.

I longed for true partnership, but what did I have to offer? Two hooks and a drawer in a cabin as gamey as Noah's Ark. Sometimes friends came to visit and stayed for months, bivouacking in one of the out buildings, but mostly I was on my own, at the mercy of the elements, inadequacy and thieves.

To balance out the loneliness and my need to be needed, I surrounded myself with dogs, cats, horses, geese, peacocks, chickens, and doves. They all roamed free by day, but had respective shelters from predators at night. Good Day Farm was also a working farm with six acres of apples from three hundred old apple trees that needed attention. Added to which there were grapefruit, lemon, avocado, apricot, pear, fig, and cherry-plum trees, grapes, a large vegetable garden, and poison oak everywhere. And did I mention rattlesnakes?

My life was one of service to this off-the-grid utopia that was as lonely as Eden. A small rental income and money from the apples paid the bills. Though my purpose of dropping out was to search for my essence, to get in touch with

sketch of cabin, Good Day Farm by Paulette Frankl

a simpler, more grounded, less consumer-based lifestyle, the fact remained that even living off the grid, life costs money. The Beatles song, "All You Need Is Love" turned love into a common currency wherein everyone was rich—so long as someone else paid the bills.

It was, of course, an intense time in the greater world. Many fled; many went to jail; many died. There was war abroad, at home, and within. I kept having a recurring vision of teetering on a tightrope above a tsunami, wobbling along with imbalance and uncertainty, searching for my essence on a thin wire with a balancing rod of determination, hoping to reach the other side intact before being swept away in the process forever.

In this crossroads of earthquakes, idealism, and grit, a lightning bolt struck. The combination of self-reliance, silence, observation, and a desperate need for artistic expression pointed me directly toward mime. All roads lead to Mecca; all mime leads to Marcel Marceau.

Chapter 5
A Force Beyond Words

In this era of the New Age, life was parodied by mime. America was experiencing a renaissance of mime. Mimes were everywhere: on the streets, at social events, performing in theaters. Much like the court jester or the fool, mimes had an otherworldly quality of wisdom about them that I found infinitely appealing. They were perceptive, expressive, athletic, graceful, and aloof.

Mime resonated with me. I had responded strongly to Marcel Carne's classic film, *Children of Paradise,* starring the great actor-mime Jean-Louis Barrault. Like Haiku, it said so much with so little, piercing straight to the heart of the matter, whatever that happened to be. So when word came to Good Day Farm that the great master of mime, Marcel Marceau, was performing at a small theater at De Anza College just an hour away, I jumped at the chance to go.

My seat was in the twenty-sixth row, terrible for mime, as the facial expressions are key. But even at that distance, I was transported into a different dimension. I couldn't believe the power of emotion evoked in me by the minimalism of Marceau's poignancy of gesture, eloquence of countenance, all with nothing: no sets, no costumes, no language. His silence was poetry personified. I was brought to tears, I rocked with laughter, and I felt pried open with pathos I didn't even know I possessed. In the poetic expression made manifest by his silence, even his thoughts became visible. He gave life to empty space. His presence filled the theater and peopled the stage of my imagination. My senses became fully ignited. I was delivered to new heights of perception and vision.

That performance became a line in my sand. It changed my life.

At intermission, I queried the ushers as to how I might get backstage. I received a no-nonsense admonition that no one was allowed backstage. No one! OK. That was clear. So when the performance was over and the audience obediently exited the front doors, I just walked against the tide, climbed onto the stage, and sought out Marceau. I inhabited the attitude that I wasn't "no one." I walked as though I *belonged* there.

It was dark in the wings. The stage crew was busy breaking down the lighting and packing up the equipment. I couldn't see much and I didn't have a clue where to go, but I felt I was being guided by a great force. Driven by this blind determination, I slammed right into him!

Stunned, I took two steps backward. Then I noticed that, standing next to him was Hans Kramer, a photographer friend who had given me my first Nikon camera, which launched me as a professional photographer. As though it were scripted, Hans introduced me to Marcel Marceau. A sudden feeling of vertigo overcame me; I thought I would faint right there at his feet.

Marcel looked directly into my soul and said, "You are an artist, aren't you?"

Shivers hit me hard. How could he know?

We made direct eye contact. Just coming off a two-hour performance, his perception was heightened to maximum aperture, while mine was also wide open because it was so dark in the wings I couldn't see a damn thing. He looked into me and I looked into him. I saw the bright orange glow of his creative core.

That exchange was enough for me to make it my purpose to meet him again. I begged Hans to help me out, but he made it clear he had no interest in setting me up with Marcel Marceau. He did, however, inform me I could reach him at the Beverly Hills Hotel.

I returned to my farm transformed. I had undergone a profound shift, though I didn't yet know what it was. I didn't know that mime would play a major role in my life, that I would study mime, become a mime, and internalize mime as the core of my creative expression. All I knew right then was that I had to see Marceau again.

Chapter 6
The Letter

On a December day after the performance in 1971, I sat on the ground under the apple trees and crafted a letter to Marcel. To say I was acutely aware that this was my only shot at getting his attention would be a gross understatement; I knew his life was a flood of fan letters. I had this vision of being in a mob scene in India, with thousands of people all jammed together, waving my hand above the multitude of heads to be noticed by a great stage deity. What could I possibly say that hadn't already been said? How could I distinguish myself from all the rest? It was my one chance-in-a-million. It just had to hit the mark. His artistry had rocked my world. Maybe, just maybe, I could make an impression on him as well.

Dear Marcel,

If I were to take your heart by surprise—quite unaware and totally off-guard—as you surprised mine from a 26th row seat of an evening together, I would whisper to you in the language of mime of the promises of the heart and how it yearns to delight.

I would invite you to follow along with me on a voyage through the fields and forests of my imagination. I would lead you through my world and be all things to you. First, perhaps, a yellow butterfly in a springtime field of red poppies, fluttering from one quivering blossom to the next, caressing the bloom with her feet and tickling the clouds with her antennae, then on to the next in dizzying pirouettes and dives, drunken with the headiness of spring. Are you there with me? Of course! For in a world without end, where else can a mime be?

Where do butterflies go when they fly out of sight? They go on a journey toward the light. They fly to the sun far beyond the clouds, and there they look upon the world as on a precious tapestry. They have a special vision, for they have wings with eyes. There, in a garden far below, stands a unicorn.

The unicorn and the garden play an interactive role. Both are sacred and eternal. And I think the unicorn would be my next role, and yours that of the garden in which she lives. The unicorn loves her garden, for it is so rich with life; the plants and creatures that live and grow in the garden love the unicorn, for she is such a delight. If you look deep into the eye of the unicorn, you will see the deep rich glow of a desert sunset, illuminating plateau after plateau of spacious landscape. She invites you to come in, inside the landscape of her eyes and to explore her many horizons; to experience her seasons, her winter, fall, and spring.

When the clouds of melancholy gather round your mind, I'd be the raindrops that cry down your cheek if you feel a sadness. And I'd caress your cheek with warm and salty touch and tickle your nose to make you smile. I would be the rain to you, the wind, and the leaves falling from the trees, and you would be the ground, and I'd nourish you and care for you and blanket you with leaves. I would be fire and water and air to you, the softness of a kitten's fur and the hardness of a lion's will that none might harm us. I would be music to you and dance and all forms of life imaginable, as you were once to me.

I offer you my hand.

Poof!
You are you and I am me. And we're not all those things at all, but just a couple of people trying to get along in this world of claws and fangs and whipped cream and make the

> *best of it. And sometimes the going's not too fun at all. And there are times when one feels that beyond the poignancy of life—which those of us who dare, reach to touch—is just an ocean of emptiness, with lots of people treading water.*
>
> *But there is more to life than that: there just has to be. And just as when I was a child I thought that the table top above my head was the horizon of the world, so now I begin to see that the four corners of everyday life do not a prison make. For to an artist, that which is visible is becomable.*
>
> *Please! Let us meet, even if only just once.*

Weeks later, the phone rang. I ran in from feeding the animals to answer it. The voice on the other end said "Allo. Eez zeese Paulette?" It was Marcel Marceau!

I was so excited, so suddenly, my solar plexus leaped up and grabbed my throat, and all I could do was burp. I was mortified. In time, he put me at ease.

His curiosity was piqued, but when he asked me to send him a photo, it was obvious he didn't remember who I was, or what I looked like, or even our encounter. Ah, the power of illusion. It draws us in, then can't remember why.

On January, 18, 1972, in response to the call, I wrote Marcel another letter.

> *Well, we have touched! You must surely be wondering about me as much as I am about you. Who is this person who, of all my many other admirers, has had the audacity and the courage to simply walk into those so carefully guarded backstage doors and play with this weary old heart? (He was neither weary nor old.)*
>
> *I wonder if you wonder how old I am? That's always such an indiscreet question to bring up with women, so I shall tell you of my own accord. When I laugh and play I am nine years old; when I make love I am a woman in her*

prime; when I sing I am a mother to her child or a child to its mother or a girl to her lover; and when I cry I am at least two thousand years old. And when I draw or write I am ageless. I am just me and all that sums up to be about 34 going on 35.

You ask for a photo. What can I send? I don't know, for I have more faces than your act. When you finish with your study of the 17 faces of mankind, you can do the thousand and forever faces of Woman.

I will send you a portrait of the way I am right now in response to you—for that which the hand creates is closest to the heart. This is from me for you. Nobody else.

I have the history of Austria in my blood—of the quaint elegance of Vienna when she was the Empress of Europe, imprinting upon the world her friendly gemutlichkeit and gracious living; of chamber concerts in Biedemeyer salons, of Straus waltzes, of the Hungarian gypsies and whatever all their allure is: horses, tambourines, violins and guitars, wild dancing, gyrating hips and lashing skirts, fire in the eyes and the crackle and heat of fire at night under a starry sky, charred meat and raw sex, and the music of Mozart. It's all there.

Then there's the Jewish bloodline: Frankl is a Jewish name, though not my family's faith. My only brush with Judaism is a penchant for rye bread. Surely Viktor Frankl, renowned author of Man's Search for Meaning, the account of his experiences in the Nazi death camps, is some relative in the woodpile, for that spelling of the name Frankl without the "e" is unusual. He hearkened from Vienna in the same era as my father, Paul T. Frankl.

I somehow sense by some weird fluke of metaphysical incarnation or cross-pollination an identity with American Indians, which although is nowhere to be found in the family records (which I've never bothered to explore), I feel very strongly in my soul, in my rapport with these people, in our "recognition" of one another. (That's when I'm two thousand years old and I relive the desert wastelands and the sorrow of a people who were conquered, genocided, misunderstood, unwanted, unused, unvalued, and trashed.)

Then there's the Mayflower side of my genetics, the Irish, English, and French offshoots who rebelled against the old feudal ways in Europe, packed their courage into their pockets, and pitted themselves against the fury of the high seas for the Promised Land. Raw courage charted their way through the storms toward the guiding light of idealism.

Oh! I forgot to mention, I was brought up by a Japanese woman whom I esteem my surrogate mother. She experienced the radiation effects of Hiroshima. When she was sent off to the Japanese concentration camps during WW II, I was packed off to be part of the Mexican gardener's family of thirteen children while my mother and father worked to make ends meet in a war-time economy. Japan: the Zen of the moment; the horizontal line and the circle. Essence, stillness, and unity. The energy we bring to each moment is the accumulative embodiment of our ancestors, of those who came before us. I represent this family of man.

Had it not been for my Austrian father, Mayflower mother, Hungarian gypsy chutzpah, Native American survival tactics, and Japanese whatever all, I would never have had the wherewithal to walk against the tide of humanity, past the crocodiles of security, after your performance to brave the forbidden dark labyrinth of your backstage to find you and meet you, so that we could imprint upon one another in that brief moment of contact.

Come! Let us touch hands that we might together breathe the infinite.

When he received the photo, he seemed relieved. We corresponded; I poured my heart into my journal. The following entry is a random, but representative example.

> *Your letter has quite overwhelmed me. You, who need no words, write so beautifully. How lucky I feel to be your innocent, so that each new discovery comes as a wonderful and unexpected gift.*
>
> *When I first saw you, so great was my surprise that I wondered if you were real at all or if you were like the moon, shining bright while in a sea of darkness, alone and out of reach.*
>
> *You ask how I live: I live what is known in the New Age jargon as an alternative lifestyle; that is, off the grid of establishment comforts and values. I live in a handmade cabin that I built with the help of friends. My son Nicholas built his own cabin near to mine. Both are small abodes, sans comforts, no indoor plumbing, only wood heat. Mine has an outdoor bathtub/shower under a redwood tree. My farm is on 74 acres in the Santa Cruz Mountains. Six acres are apple trees; I tend and lend a hand in keeping the orchard healthy and producing for the yearly harvest. The first year, four of us harvested 42 tons of apples: that's circa ten tons each. That's a lot of back-breaking hard work. It overlooks a lovely valley with lakes and orchards and redwood forests and eventually the ocean.*
>
> *My life is a combination of hard work, a lot of introspection, and learning to live in harmony with myself and nature. Sometimes the challenge is daunting, such as when the roof of my cabin blows off in a storm or when the road washes out or when animals get eaten or maimed by predators. I paint and write and take photographs and tend the animals and cook and keep the fire going all night long in winter. I have a small income that pays the bills. It*

is an experience in personal growth. So as to the question, "What do I do?" I do whatever needs doing and there's always something. Life is abundantly full of needs and gifts.

"Do I like youth and beauty?" you ask.
Of course I like youth and beauty, especially to look at, but beauty I see in everything, and as for youth, I prefer depth.

We spoke of our images of each other. My images of you are few and simple. The first image I have of you comes from my impressions of my twenty-sixth-row seat at your performance. Realize, I could only see your silhouette at that distance. I could hardly see your face at all, as I had no opera glasses. Still, even at that, I found your poetry so perfect: so simple, so tender, so beautifully humorous, sane, and yet so filled with melancholy. Your language was exactly that of my own had I been able to express myself so perfectly. I was astounded. I felt like I was witnessing my conscious

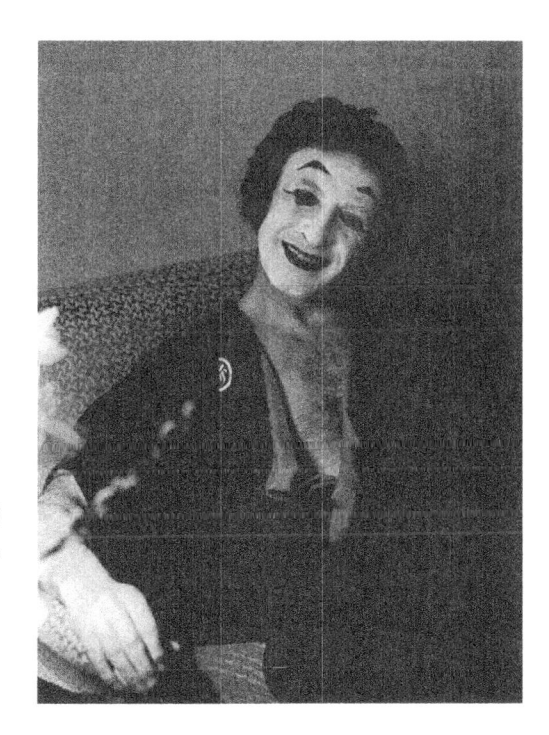

Marcel Marceau, 1972
PHOTO: PAULETTE FRANKL

The Letter | 43

Paulette Frankl, 1972
PHOTO: SUZ CAMERON

> *counterpart. And the next impression was when I met you for that brief minute backstage. I registered two things: the aliveness of the glow of your volcano in your eyes, and your truly beautiful humbleness. Such a rare combination!*
>
> *I love talking to you. I hear in your voice the ringing of bells.*
>
> *You ask if I am excited about our meeting. What a question! I am consumed with joy! And at the same time I feel a certain sadness, for it is at once a beginning and an end: a beginning of something new, and the end of my life as it was, because I already feel the shift of a new paradigm. There is always sadness in joy. It is inevitable.*

Finally, a double act of bald-faced bravery ensued: Marcel invited me to join him in Chicago and Detroit for the last leg of his American tour, and I accepted. It was winter 1972. I was 34. Marcel was 49.

Chapter 7
On Wings of Desire

Earth shifted on its axis.

I was in no way ready for an encounter of this magnitude. I was a California hippie, divorced mother, living on a farm. I was also the daughter of a world-famous Austrian designer, a graduate from Stanford University in art and languages, and a world traveler, but I didn't have a background in theater. I knew enough to know that I had taken on more than I could handle. I didn't really know anything about the history of mime and even less about the background of Marcel Marceau. Our common thread was that we were both artists seeking essence. I spoke French and he spoke English. We were both citizens of the world and children of the muse. I had reached out to him and his hand reached back to touch mine. The mistress of fantasy had been touched by the master of illusion. I continued to be driven by a force far greater than reason.

I left my farm in the hands of Dennis (our relationship was on the rocks by then), packed for come-what-may, and flew into the icy grip of the Windy City in winter. I had no clothes suitable for a winter of Chicago's caliber, not even the mentality of what would be needed: no hat, no scarf, no gloves, no long underwear—just raw determination. Cinderella had managed to manifest her prince, but I had no fairytale godmother to fund the ball or the airfare, and I certainly had no wardrobe consultant or the purse-strings for a gracious entrée into the high society of Chicago's theater set. What was I thinking? What on earth does a country girl wear on a week-long tryst with the world's most famous mime, with barely enough money to feed the chickens?

With what little money I could muster, I had a full-length velvet cape of my own design made, with appliquéd flowers on the nape and shoulder, the petals of which tumbled down the back of the cape. Actually, the dark green velvet fabric had formerly served as a curtain, and there was a sun streak down the back that the petals helped to conceal. Black velvet pants and a sheer lace top completed the effect. Well, almost. I ran out of money when it came to the shoes, so I had to make do with my best farm boots. I coined it a new look in fashion: delicate and tough.

On February 6, I wrote in my journal:

This plane is like a floating hotel lobby. It's my first experience in a 747: IMMENSE! Seats in all directions as far as the eye can see, with a view of a South Sea's atoll on the wall and Mexican music piped through the ceiling. There is everything but the key to your room.

There are so many people boarding that a receptionist met me halfway down the corridor of the boarding gate to direct me to a specialized desk. Size. America is size. There is room for everything here—even a 747. Where else would such a giant have ever been conceived? I suppose the movie is on wide-angle screen. I love America for its large-scale insanity, for its monstrosities; I love America for having the size to accommodate such things.

The weather is cloudy: thunderheads and sunshine. I have the feeling that when this monster of the skies thunders through the clouds on its mechanized flight, the impact of its size and weight and volume on all that delicate air will change the very weather itself.

The loudspeaker is on. The captain is introducing the crew. When he introduces the stewardesses, the passengers applaud, like a TV audience.

I am handed a coil of plastic-coated wire. Earphones for the entertainment. Now jazz is throbbing from the ceiling. We are ready for takeoff. The engines are on and it smells like we're all going to be gassed with our seatbelts on. Maybe it's just the modern-day form of mass extermination. Maybe these planes never really go anywhere at all. Maybe we all just bought in to get away from it all once and forever. Some people sleep. The man next to me briefs himself on his business matters ahead. Others read the paper. What a way to go!

We are moving now. Is it us moving or is it the rest of the airport that's just passing by the window? The fumes pour in at an astonishing rate. Worse than a smoky fireplace.

The stewardess has thorns for eyelashes, sharp enough to draw blood, and bloated lacquered lips of a violent red. Outside everything is gray.

Here we go.

The jazz music never misses a beat as this giant creature rushes upward in a soaring lunge for height and speed. The good sky supports it as we tear through the clouds into a silent sea of billowy white clouds.

Feeling as though I was rocketing out of orbit to a different planet on wings of desire, I arrived in Chicago an exhausted wreck. The stress of the trip and this ordeal of manifesting fantasy into reality was written all over my face.

A large bouquet of long-stem yellow roses awaited me in the hotel, with a note from Marcel welcoming me and instructing me to meet him at the theater. I was not accustomed to receiving flowers from international superstars (or anyone else, for that matter), and I burst into tears, which added to the puffiness of my already pasty appearance.

I was to meet Marcel in the backstage lounge, where he was resting between his matinee and evening performances. There was not enough time for a restorative nap and hot bath, but just enough time to slap a mud mask on my face in hopes of a miraculous transformation. The mud was in powder form, needing only water for reconstitution. It messed up my bathroom something frightful, but I figured no one was going to see it but me.

Mercifully, the theater was a short distance from the hotel, for when I stepped out into the icy maw of that Chicago winter in my velvet and lace, the merciless cold took a severe bite out of my fantasy wherein weather conditions with Marcel Marceau could only be balmy and sublime.

Chapter 8

Chasing a Mime, Catching an Illusion

Marcel stood up to greet me.

He was still in whiteface from his matinee performance. A black Japanese kimono covered his costume. I was startled by his short stature and knocked aback by his pungent bad breath. (I later learned he never ate between performances, because involving his digestive system with food interfered with his timing onstage. I thought, "Fine, but some water with lemon juice sure would have helped.") A bowl of fruit was on the table, obviously untouched.

As I reached my arm around his torso to deliver a French kiss-kiss on his cheeks, I felt his squishy flesh seep between my fingers from his tight body corset. Suddenly, I realized that the corset gave him his forever-young profile onstage. He seemed older than I had fancied. He had told me he was forty-six, but it turns out he had taken a little artistic license. "Never let the truth get in the way of a good story," he was fond of saying.

We stared at each other, stunned in the headlights of the collision of illusion with reality. There we suddenly were, face to face! His whiteface makeup was peeling, accentuating the deep lines on his expressive face. The extreme white of the pancake makeup made his teeth appear jaundice-yellow. This was a face I had loved from the twenty-sixth row, but had never seen in the light of day at close range.

I stared at his features with a mixture of awe and horror.

His long nose was classically French; his sensitive lips, with red lipstick lined in black, and his strong cleft chin were a handsome combination. The broad black eyeliner with the Egyptian-stylized tear under each eye, no longer impeccable after undergoing the heat of the stage lights from a previous performance, was now both startling and scary. The open kimono and low cut of his costume revealed his pleasantly hairy chest. Broad sideburns framed his face.

Meanwhile, Marcel's radar vision took me in, every inch of me. I felt him peeling me like an orange. His intensity had been exciting to me onstage, but now it made me feel naked, insecure, over-exposed, and judged. He seemed to register my every thought and emotion. My overload of conflicting reactions surely gave him a lot to process! I was horrified at the thought. He must have realized he was coming on too strong for from that moment on, he focused his attention on the floor instead, repeating "How was your flight?"

"Marcel! You've asked me this question three times."

My mind searched desperately, as if for something lost, for the missing link as to why I was here, in this hot seat, surrounded by all-consuming flames of personal inadequacy while burning alive at the same time as drowning in a rising sea of silence. This was hyper-perceptivity run amuck! He was speechless, and I was at a loss for what to say. What was I to do? Was I supposed to make *him* feel comfortable? For God's sake! I was dumbstruck just to be in his presence.

He continued staring downward like a young boy, as though some magical hand would appear and save him or a trap door would open and mercifully swallow him whole. How much time had passed in this interminable discomfort? Minutes? Hours? Decades? I could sense myself aging.

We were no longer two people in a small room but two solitary and separate entities, each isolated in the grip of silence, the silence of vacancy. In the stranglehold of our inability to converse, ambient sounds intensified, reminiscent of those awful moments in horror films when the sound of a beating heart encroaches from every direction in an amplified metronome of dread.

After what seemed like an eternity, Marcel slowly looked up at me, giving me direct eye contact, and said, "It's because when I'm in the presence of true beauty, I always feel humble and at a loss for words."

Oh my God! My tormentor was filled with flattery!

I was stunned. Here we were, face to face, in the shock of each other, in the push-pull of conflicting reactions, with a week of togetherness ahead in which to answer to this magnetic manifestation totally based on illusion. It was a hard reckoning with reality.

It is miraculous how something, as if on cue, always intervenes, steps in, and slaps us with a cold wet rag to break the spell. In this case, it came in the form of the stage manager, notifying Marcel that it was time to get ready for his grand-finale performance. It was a godsend of relief for us both.

"I play for you tonight," he said, in his particular high-pitched voice with his French accent.

I was ushered to a perfect fourth-row center seat in the beautiful theater. As I sank into the plush velvet, I noticed that the theater was packed, a sold-out performance with standing room only. This was Marcel's closing night in Chicago, with the glitterati turned out to the nines, along with students and families with children. Theater lovers of every sort buzzed with the anticipation of experiencing the art of the great mime.

The house lights dimmed. A startling succession of loud thumping noises backstage commanded the audience's attention. A hush fell over the magnificent, multi-tiered theater as darkness enveloped the audience.

The curtain parted.

For an instant, the darkness expanded in scope and dimension into an infinity devoid of light and sound.

Then!

A burning beam of white light slowly came into focus in the center of this immensity of black, revealing the presence of Marcel Marceau. Dressed entirely in white, he appeared like a human column of light: at once rooted and weightless, with one arm raised in a proclamation of presence. Staring directly at everyone and no one, he drew in the attention of his audience with a tidal force. A shock of goose bumps shivered my arms as I felt myself being engulfed by his spell.

Then Marcel seemed to dematerialize, replaced in the spotlight by his assistant, Pierre Verry. Pierre stood statue-still, holding a sizable white placard at arm's length to one side, which bore the name of the first skit. He wore a pink-and-black satin costume, with a tunic, tights, and a plume on his large hat. His tights revealed the well-defined muscles of his powerful legs, necessary for the art of mime. His costume was of an old-world European theatrical style and era. It was in stark contrast to Marcel's streamlined costume that was timeless. Even from my seat at a close distance, I couldn't discern if Pierre was live or a mannequin. He didn't even blink in the glare of the stage lights as he stood frozen in his discipline of stillness, holding the large placard in his outstretched arms. Another wink of the stage light, and Pierre, too, vanished.

In his place stood Marcel.

He took us into the wind, as he battled the power of an imaginary gale, pulling forward while being pushed backward, giving the illusion of moving ahead while remaining in place. This style of movement was originally created by Jean-Louis Barrault, then adapted by Marceau, from which Michael Jackson later fashioned his moonwalk.

In another vignette, Marcel became a mask maker, crafting a series of Kabuki-esque masks depicting expressions of power, fear, sorrow, and laughter. He then switched into the role of the mask wearer, who frivolously flaunts expressions, masquerades meaning, and parades transformative power and corresponding body language. Suddenly, Marcel changed pace, producing one masked expression after another in dizzying succession until one mask stuck, like instant paralysis. Laughter.

Now the laughing face became its opposite: an outcry of distress in the guise of joviality. Marcel struggled desperately to remove this mask of laughter that entombed his inner despair. His neck muscles corded. He bent over backward. His shoulders heaved. He leaned with his arms dangling limp, helpless to overcome this disfiguring entrapment, unable to liberate himself from this mocking misconception of joy. I was riveted as he took an imaginary chisel and struck a blow to his masked brow. The grip of the mask lessened. Marcel had damaged it enough to be able to budge it. With elbows raised high and fingers grasping the rim of the imaginary mask like fingered hooks, he slowly, ever so slowly, began to raise the mask from his face. His chin quivered with fearful anxiety, while the rest of his expression remained motionless. In a maneuver of dazzling intricacy, Marcel exhibited a breathtaking display of facial-muscle isolation: The lower half of his face was animated in the fearful struggle, while the remaining upper half was frozen in the masked laughter. At one precise point, his face convulsed with the agony of crying while grimacing with laughter. By the time the mask was fully removed, Marcel's face was as though naked, devoid of expression, with only a haunting stare into the void, reflecting the moment of truth.

(Later, I read a comment Marcel made about this piece in an interview. "Today, people put on masks all the time. What is their real face? And suddenly the mask reveals an unmasked face in its nudity and speaking the moment of truth, which is extreme solitude.")

His diverse program, devoid of words, but rich in emotion, held his audience spellbound in the tragi-comedy of the human condition, with an eloquence of gesture that was neither overdone nor underplayed. Marcel held his audience in the palm of his hand for more than two hours. At the end, he brought down the house. The waves of applause went on and on. The audience didn't want to release him.

I was dumbstruck anew by his power of emotional projection. All my chakras came alive, stimulated and played out. The performance was a perfect end to my long and difficult day. I was done in. The farmer in me was ready to close the barn door, turn off the lights, and hit the sack.

But to urban-night-owl Marcel, the night was just beginning! There was a farewell dinner party and celebrations. All of Chicago was enamored with the French mime. He had taken the Windy City by storm.

Chapter 9
All in a Day's Work

Marcel reappeared, strutting offstage in his street clothes. He walked with the long and confident stride of a conqueror. From a distance, I thought he was a woman! His large, full-length fur coat and tall Russian fur hat were like nothing I'd ever seen on a man, or on anything short of a yak, for that matter. He looked utterly effeminate. I went into shock nouveau. I'd never been with a man who wasn't a hunk, and here I was with the man of my dreams, my Prince Charming, who was beyond androgynous: he was surreal. His fluidity of movement was more like an aquatic invertebrate than anything human. His flesh as was soft as a jellyfish. Those hands were liquid light. He had the body of a dancer, lithe and toned. His legs were powerful coiled springs. Those legs could dip him in and out of a backbend all the way down to the floor and back up again, or slide sideways out from under him into the splits and then return him to a standing position, with the apparent weightlessness of a puppet being drawn by strings from above. But his arms had never lifted anything heavier than his overcoat. They had strength but were not manly.

To my chagrin and confusion, those qualities that I found most compelling about him onstage were perplexing to me offstage. Onstage he was composed, self-contained, and in full command. Offstage he was hyped, a nonstop monologue, a windmill of words and gestures. I watched, for the second time that evening a hostage to my own stunned silence. I felt myself shrink before the immensity of it all: his presence, charisma, fame, fans, and androgyny. I felt myself falling and shrinking, excruciatingly out of place, uncomfortable in my own skin. I had to do some quick self-hypnosis to recover my center in the presence of his all-consuming magnetism.

Marcel escorted me to his waiting car, where we were chauffeured to a high-society party. The room was an aviary of Chicago's birds of paradise, and Marcel was all a-twitter. He schmoozed the divas of his day like the conqueror that he was. I don't remember saying a word, though my presence as his date did receive a lot of raised-eyebrow glances that were statements unto themselves. The hostess commented "Oh, isn't she cute?" in a voice dripping with sarcasm. I felt like a stage prop, something dragged along for embellishment. It didn't help that the guests were Chicago's posh theater and dance set, turned out in the finest couture that money could buy. Not only did I feel out of place, but I didn't recognize one diva from another. And there I was, in my outlandish velvet, lace, and farm boots. Luckily, it was 1972, when a hippie could hang uptown or downtown, with rattlesnakes in apple orchards or on Lakeshore Drive with Marcel Marceau. I held my head high and assumed the air of someone who was wearing the cutting-edge latest in hip couture. I carried it off, meeting the disapproving looks I received with my only weapon: audacious disdain. I eyed them up and down as they did me, as though their designer clothing was sadly outdated.

Oddly enough, the situation at hand was one of life's reversals of fortune. My father was a world-class Viennese designer. Paul T. Frankl was the product of talent, culture, and wealth in the era when Vienna was Queen of Europe and her subjects waltzed to the music of Strauss. My grandfather, whom I never knew, owned about five hundred acres of downtown Vienna. The family mansion on the Auhoff Strasse was three hundred yards from the original Schonbrun summer Palace of Emperor Franz Josef, a frequent visitor to my grandmother Emma's Sunday kaffe klatsches. He clippity-clopped over for coffee at the Frankl family estate in his horse-drawn carriage along the elegant, tree-lined, cobblestone street. There were stories of how my father's brothers enjoyed the services of women-for-hire, then paid them in mink coats. The family fortune vanished overnight with the fall of the Austrian Empire and the devaluation of the shilling, along with gross mismanagement and squandering by the decadent brothers.

When the crash came, my father gathered up all his money in a wheelbarrow and marched right to a travel agent, where he bought a one-way ticket to New York City and the Land of the Free. There, he began anew as a nobody, free to succeed or fail on his merits, not his family fortune or pedigree. His new life in the New World as a furniture designer and interior decorator brought him both success and failure. He summited the highest pinnacle as one of the founders of the Art Deco movement and the creator of skyscraper furniture. He established his legacy as one of the premier furniture designers and interior decorators in America, but died riddled with money worries, unable to get work.

As a young child during the war, I recall Sunday gatherings of geniuses at our charming caretaker's cottage on the Vanderlip Estate of the Palos Verdes peninsula. I sat on the generous lap of Charles Laughton as he read passages from the Bible, his booming voice resounding like the roar and echo of waves rolling into shore after lunch in the languid California afternoons. Charlie Chaplin, Katharine Hepburn, and Jascha Heifetz were clients of my father and visitors at our Sunday lunches. Frank Lloyd Wright and Cliff May were peers and close friends. I recall the guests arriving around eleven in the morning. Cocktails were followed by a work-of-art lunch with lively conversation, after which everyone fell asleep in my father's wonderful furniture or on the hammock overlooking the ocean. Around four in the afternoon, cocktails and conversation resumed, and leftovers fed everyone until late at night. We visited with his friends Diego Rivera and silversmith William Spratling when we traveled to Mexico. I took luminaries for granted and, from my limited exposure to life within the glass walls of my petri dish, I assumed all grownups were like that. It was perhaps that deep longing to return to the scintillating luminescence of genius energy that motivated me to seek, and place myself in the presence of Marcel Marceau.

My father died at seventy-one in California, eaten alive with cancer and money worries. His lifestyle was out of balance with his

All in a Day's Work | 57

income. Cancelled medical insurance gutted what remained of the coffers. Times had changed; his exquisite taste and great style were no longer in demand. Sick, depressed, and nearly destitute, he no longer had the energy to begin anew. My mother died a year later. Just as I was of an age to leave the nest, my world crumbled out from under me. I quickly married.

Marcel's and my background had more in common than I realized at the time. We both lost our fathers when we were just turning twenty, coming of age. We were both traumatized by death at an early age, forced to grow up fast. And we both created mini-utopias where we lived. Beauty was our antidote to the pain and cruelties of life.

In the days when Marcel studied theater, a career in acting was considered to be outside the perimeter of social acceptability. A person of the theater belonged to the brethren of bohemians, a dangerous fraternity known for its unbridled, ungoverned behavior, immoral values, dubious sexuality, unpredictable social manners, and above all, an artistic lifestyle synonymous with starvation.

Times had changed. Here we were together, Marcel and me, in 1972, in generation-gap New Age America at a high-society party in Chicago. I was the thoroughbred turned hippie; Marcel was the son of a kosher butcher turned world-famous entertainer. He had ratcheted himself up by his bootstraps and had now achieved international acclaim. I had turned my back on my past and chosen instead the New Age values of oneness without fortune or rank. Rank, class, and beauty were no longer matters of money, status, or physical appearance, but inner comportment and consciousness.

We were at a high-society party in Chicago. Marcel's cultural background in theater was infinitely refined and sophisticated. But here I was among a milieu of society that I had flat-out rejected ever since my father's death in 1958. Though I'd been born with a silver spoon in my mouth and grown up with nursemaids all my privileged life, they were the people with whom I had bonded and grown to love. I spit out that silver spoon and took up their cause, their foreignness and hardships. I felt much more of a kinship with them and their plights than I did with the clients of my father's world. My affiliation was with the common people.

Perhaps that is why I was so taken by Marcel's character Bip. It was really Bip who spoke to my heart and soul.

Bip with his battered burlap opera hat, symbolizing culture without status or wealth.

Bip the dreamer of a better world, the romantic, the poet and lover of flowers.

Bip the bungler, the tough little survivor who never gave up, the character whose struggle spoke to my own heart.

It was really in search of Bip that I had traveled across the country; it was for Bip that I fashioned my cape from a curtain. Bip would understand the improper shoes. Bip would empathize with my malaise at this social party of movers and shakers and grande dames. Did he not suffer the frivolities of these people every single night on stage? Wasn't "The Society Party" one of his skits?

Bip would approve of my boldness in reaching out to be with Marcel and my awkwardness in actually manifesting this dream; of wanting desperately to fit in, to belong, and never quite getting it right; of saying the wrong thing; of wearing the wrong thing; of having hair that was not professionally coiffed or dyed; of not wearing makeup. Bip would sympathize with being judged at every turn by the dragons that guarded Marcel's inner circle, and by Marcel himself, the grand master of his own illusion. Marcel, the man, was a stranger to me. He bore no resemblance to Bip. Where the hell was Bip when I needed him?

Around four-thirty in the morning, Marcel escorted me to my hotel room. We were scheduled to depart at seven-thirty a.m. sharp for Detroit. I was so tired the ground beneath my feet no longer seemed solid. I waded through my fatigue into my spinning room on rubber legs in hot tar. A high-pitched hummmm in my ears was decidedly not the chimes of celestial harmonies, but rather of malfunctioning circuitry desperately in need of repose. My mouth tasted like the bottom of a birdcage. My body was chilled lead.

Upon entering my room, we exchanged what I thought was a mannerly goodnight embrace. Little did I realize it was the match to his tinderbox! It became one of those moments where everything changed in an instant. The entire evening suddenly veered off course.

Just as I was about to cave in to total exhaustion, Marcel jumped me. No warning, no lead-in, no seduction, no kissing, no foreplay, just sheer carnal lust. The fox was in the hen house and I was the object of his feeding frenzy. I was in no way prepared for the impact of that initial sexual encounter.

First, it seemed so out of character. Marcel had been the quintessential old-world European gentleman up until then. But he was, after all, the universal master of a thousand personas. Had I somehow missed noticing his Marquis de Sade? Surely even he would not bypass foreplay! Perhaps Marcel thought that the gift of two dozen long-stem roses, my own hotel room, two performances that day, including dedicating Chicago's closing performance to me, followed by a sustained standing ovation and countless curtain calls, being the toast of the town and the darling of Chicago's high society *all added up to* the foreplay! Now he was ready to cut right to the chase. Sex!

His coat hit the floor along with the rest of his clothes. Being the quick-change artist he was, he was fully naked before I could even begin to grasp what was happening. I stood aghast, staring at his sturdy erect panpipe between his powerful furry legs. I guessed it was his way of showing me that he was *not* an old man, and *certainly* not a woman, nor an old-world gentleman either, but rather, lust personified! I was pleased to discover that not all parts of his body were equally subject to the aging process. The family jewels seemed to remain taut and forever young, immune from the ravages of time.

He seemed so electrically charged that I dared not touch anything. His urgency was overwhelming. I couldn't wrap my mind around his unbridled passion. Was he role-playing the fire-in-the-belly gypsy from one of my letters? Obviously, he'd presented me with an evening of utmost refinement; was this now the raw-meat part? Or was this the Zen archery of mime, wherein the arrow and the target become one? In truth, it seemed totally inappropriate and thoroughly out of touch, after a long evening of almost no personal interaction. I didn't realize at the time that Marcel was not one to *inter*-act. He was a one-man show!

His assumptions ran unchecked, since I was too dumbstruck to openly express any objection in a manner that would not be as equally offensive as his advances.

He was all over me.

No slow titillating caress that stirs the deeper senses to awakening and turns the tendrils of sensuality toward the touch like a plant toward sunlight. No tenderness that jumpstarts the flow of juices from the lotus that sets alight the fragrance of the hot and hairy swamp of desire where the slime meets the divine. No "take your time and do it right" on this first night together. No! None of that.

Instead, Marcel was furiously working me over—a blind man urgently fingering my flesh to find the "on" switch for the complex control panel on this body of a woman. He was even violating the first commandment of all performers: "Quit while you're ahead. Leave your audience wanting more!"

Marcel had clearly crossed all boundaries of socially acceptable behavior. He was trying to extinguish his personal brushfire, the burning consumption of an older man lusting for a younger woman's body, with a blazing urgency to finish fast enough to get some sleep before takeoff in a few hours.

Once again, I found myself in a moment of reckoning with reality. Naturally, it was my nature to want to please the man of my dreams, and in the heart of my fantasy, Marcel was a god of unparalleled proportions. But my only experience with gods had been in books and on film screens. This awakening was illusion spinning madly out of control.

Marcel was naked, but his attempt to liberate me from my clothing was another matter altogether. My lace top fit like a well-spun cocoon with no zipper or fastener. It was one of those tight-fitting things that needed careful attention to wriggle in and out of without destroying the delicacy of the antique lace. For a moment, I feared that my one and only outfit suitable for evening wear was going to meet its ruin on our very first night together. I jabbed him an elbow of interference in order to do the job of removing my own clothing.

While my face and upper body disappeared into the struggle with my lace top, Marcel busied himself with the removal of my velvet pants and foxy undergarments. He flung my lace bra and thong onto the floor. They ended up sprawled atop the fur neck of his caveman coat in what appeared at a glance to be an unlikely combination of the delicate with a beast. I myself was also soon on the floor in a full-body-roll with an alligator.

I recall no dialogue, just an inner shrieking of sensations. His mouth, his tongue, his hands—those same hands that had been liquid light on stage—were now ten-fingered, high-voltage electric charges that blew all my fuses. They were everywhere at once, tweaking, vibrating, forcing entry into an oyster that wasn't ready to be shucked and sucked. I could in no way keep up with his rapacious appetite for sex, let alone connect. I tried desperately just to hang on, to survive this sensory onslaught.

It wasn't that I hadn't imagined having sex with Marcel; of course I had! It's just that in my fantasy, it wasn't anything like this. I had fancied the magic of mutual caress, tender fingertips, loving touch, appreciation at the newness of our naked bodies discovering, arousing, and finding fit with each other. I imagined moving together—myself and this man who was so into his body—with grace and agility, our passions journeying together in the flow of two rivers joining to form a single waterfall, merging ever more into oneness until we were pure energy in motion.

But in reality, Marcel wasn't of that ilk. He was all about control. It seemed to me that even the act of sex was all about him! He was clearly directing the show. He was more interested in my affirmation of him as a lover than in experiencing a connection in love-making together.

"Do you like me?"

"Are you excited by me?"

"Is it good?"

"Are you climaxing?"

And here I was, unable to determine if I was coming or going!

He demanded that I surrender myself to him completely. "Don't hold back!" he insisted as he tunneled into my body and plundered me.

In a brief moment when a sensation of pure pleasure overrode this sensory riot, I let out a moan of erotic joy.

"Louder! LOUDER!" he commanded.

What the hell! Was he orchestrating my orgasm? That, finally, killed it. Shot down in midair. I had to curb myself from expressing the irony of this master of silence demanding that my moans and groans be heard in the farthest reaches of the vast hotel hallway. Was he still playing to an audience? To whom was this show directed? Did he expect hotel doors to fly open and strangers to applaud from out of the darkness when it was over? Was this to be his last ovation of this interminable evening?

(I didn't know at the time that to Marcel, all of life was a stage.)

My mind and body were at war with one another. My mind took command in the dreadful disconnect that every woman knows only too well. As I went into "fake-it" mode, I heard myself think, "What's going on here? Is this an audition?" How could this god on stage, who was so into his body, be so insecure and out of touch in the bedroom? My mind grasped for survival instructions and understood that to walk out onto this limb with the world's most famous mime was above all to be adaptive—instantly adaptive, come what may. It was my first bold step into trial by fire. I had to be nimble not to get burned.

Though the floor never felt so hard, and I never thought anyone could have so many knees, I wasn't about to be outdone as a sport to the challenge. I gave him what he wanted. I writhed in pretzel poses. I panted in feigned abandon.

Then I was thrown onto the bed, and I went into a newly learned, belly-dance abdominal roll that I had practiced to perfection. It was a very difficult move to pull off lying down, and I was quite proud to have mastered it and be able to finally flaunt something of my own physical prowess to him. I could motor those ab muscles around in any and all directions, like a snake—with hiccups.

Marcel stopped abruptly, reared up like a cobra, curled his lip, and hissed, "Love me with your heart and soul, not your *technique*!"

My blood froze. How could I make a comeback from that? I might well have asked, "Where's *your* heart and soul, maestro?" But instead, I died a little, feeling I had failed yet again. I reached to recoup the moment with a loving caress to his face and head.

"Don't touch my head," he growled, baring his yellow teeth, as he recoiled.

That was when I realized he was wearing a wig!

The spark sputtered and died. Marcel huffed off into my bathroom. Suddenly, the voice in my mind cried out, "No! *Not* the bathroom!" For there—all over the floor and sink and mirror—were traces, splatterings, and footprints of mud from my face pack earlier that afternoon.

I died yet again.

I had so wanted this initial evening to go beautifully. In Marcel's momentary absence, I realized that I was suffering from the shock of shattered illusion: the shock of pursuing Marcel's whiteface to the far reaches of America in the dead of winter; the shock of the real Marceau up close, older, shorter, reeking of bad breath, wearing a corset and a wig and looking like my grandmother, with the flesh of a jellyfish, totally androgynous, effeminate yet brutishly macho, demanding, controlling, and judgmental, totally full of himself, the absolute darling of the theater and dance world (with which I had nothing in common), and more consumed in showing off to me than in being with me, jumping my bones at an hour in my farmer's frame of reference when the rooster was beginning to crow the dawning of a new day. I was overloaded with sensations, all right, none of which were passion. I just wanted to escape and crash. I would kill for sleep. This tryst with the great Marcel Marceau was turning out to be the death of a thousand cuts.

CHAPTER 10

Phoenix Rising

My alarm rang before I had a chance to sink into desperately needed deep sleep. As I surfaced to my senses, I realized that I was in a strange hotel room in Chicago and that I had just spent fourteen hours with the legendary Marcel Marceau!

Daylight burned my eyes.

Emotionally, I felt like I'd been in a rock tumbler, tossed about by the conflicting forces of illusion and reality. I was awake, but was I really? I took stock.

The hotel room seemed real enough. The bedding was all a-tumble from the upheavals of last night's wrestling match. My clothes were still strewn all over the floor.

Part of me was directly living the experience while another part was observing myself from a different seat of perception. I was reaching for my journal to write down these first impressions before they became eclipsed by the next round, when there was a urgent knock on my door.

It was Marcel, all bushy-tailed, wanting more sex! "NO!" I thought. "Mercy!"

I quickly hid the evidence of my journal under the covers and hoped he wouldn't take the liberty to climb into bed and discover it or sit on its hard cover with its pokey corners. Who knew what he'd do if he busted me red-handed?

Meanwhile, I was once again torn between loving his spontaneity and wanting to please him, and needing time to compose myself after last night's mauling. I couldn't get my bearings in his immediacy, his all-consuming presence. I couldn't even find myself in this out-of-context role I was playing: was I just another groupie keeping a diary or was I indeed a candidate for something authentic, something real? And if so, what did "real" look like in his world of illusion? Could I still ask him to sign my program? Could I take notes? Could I take pictures? Who was I? I'd never been in this position before. His world was all about him. Or was that too an illusion?

The only thing I knew for sure was that the plane for Detroit was leaving at seven-thirty a.m., and no way would I be late on this first morning with a man whose timing was impeccable.

Awaiting his car to take us to the airport, I stared at all the luggage with which Marcel traveled. For someone who toured the world non-stop, he seemed to be schlepping most of that world right along with him. Those were the days before airports were such a dreadful experience, when traveling with a lot of baggage was not an unthinkable nightmare and unspeakable expense, providing you had a village of sherpas to handle it. I presumed that his Coco Chanel suitcases contained things he couldn't live without: clothes for every kind of weather and occasion, special accouterments such as wigs, gifts of all sizes for and from loved ones of all measures, objects d'art, trinkets, even a library of books. I knew that his costumes and everything involved with his show were handled by his team. My own canvas shoulder bag, only slightly eaten in a few places by farm mice, looked exactly as I felt: like it didn't belong. But there we stood, on the curbstone of this beautiful hotel with our baggage, physical and emotional, waiting to be transported away to more time and greater intimacy together.

On the flight to Detroit, Marcel confessed that he was terrified of flying. To take his mind off the unnerving turbulence, he entertained me with stories in a combination of languages: English, French, German, and Italian, with a little Japanese thrown in. Marcel loved to talk as much as he loved silence. In fact, once he got started, there was no stopping him. I was transfixed by his expressions and gestures. Never in my life was the experience of being strapped to a seat so filled with fantasy. His ability to stylize and transform the mundane into the phantasmagorical was limitless. My ego—clamoring to be seen or heard, or fighting for footing was petty and insignificant compared to his imagination and expression. All that was required

sketch by Paulette Frankl   *sketch by Marcel Marceau*

of me was learning to relax and enjoy his presence. I was discovering a new kind of togetherness.

In Detroit, Marcel booked us a suite together. It was a leap of faith on his part. A shift of comfort with each other had occurred on that bumpy plane ride.

I remember noticing, in the first day or two in Detroit, the respect with which Marcel treated those whose stations in life might be considered invisible, such as elevator operators and doormen. He, who had reached the top of stardom, always acknowledged them and expressed his thanks, no matter how menial their services; he made them feel noticed and appreciated. He took nothing and no one for granted. I couldn't help reflect that I too was one of those invisible people reaching toward him, toward his light of recognition, and he reached to touch my hand, my heart, and pull me out of the shadows. In his invitation he'd said we'd go to museums, paper the hotel-room walls with our art, fill the room with flowers. Reality did manage to accommodate the fantasy, somewhat. Fans sent flowers; we also gave flowers to each other, and we did sketch each other. But mostly the demands of Marcel's professional life took precedence. By day, the man was a hostage to the box-office idol. He had meetings with his agent and his brother Alain, who doubled as his business manager. He posed for photographers. He sat with writers, producers, publishers, reporters, and interviewers. He consulted with his stage manager. He had squabble-fests about money. For such a great artist, the wolf of money matters never stopped biting at his heels.

Then there was the endless phone time. As Marcel was almost always on tour, entire continents of his time were spent on the phone. Calls with his children (Marcel was between marriages at this time) and extended family. Calls about future projects—tours, books, films.

And then there was the fan mail. Mail to be read, answered, kept, discarded.

It seemed that everyone on Earth wanted a piece of him. He seemed to live in a sea of piranhas all tearing away mouthfuls of his time. Still, he thrived on the attention. It was his oxygen, but it was too much of a good thing. Marcel was not one to say no. His every minute was gobbled up.

By the time he finally emerged from the demands of the world, it was time to perform. Marcel performed every night except Monday, and twice on Sunday. I was always comped the best seat in the house. I never tired of watching him onstage. It was my Darsham, my sacrosanct time of sitting at the feet of the great master and absorbing his teachings. Though the program was almost always the same, I discovered new levels of depth to his work each time. His language of silence was crafted with such crisp precision that it conveyed an immensity of meaning. It was the Haiku of silence. I never ceased to be amazed at his ability to imply so much with merely a gesture of his hand or the tilt of his head or a twist of his mouth.

On the other hand, there was a comforting sameness night after night. His repertoire was huge, but he rarely deviated from the reliable favorites that assured box-office success. Even the reporter's questions tended to be the same.

Being a fly on his wall gave me a taste of what it was like to be a performer of his caliber. He had to remain in performance-perfect condition. Nothing about his life was haphazard. He couldn't dine in places he didn't know. He didn't drink, smoke, or eat between performances. Dinner was never before midnight. Basically, nothing he did upset or threatened his focus or his perfect timing onstage. He couldn't afford to get sick, to blow an emotional fuse, or to miss a show; he had no back-up or understudy. There was only one Marcel Marceau. Thus, he avoided anything that might upset the controlled circumstances of his life. That was probably why he guarded his emotions so carefully. There was no room in his life for flights of fancy or crash-and-burn landings. It was bad enough that he had to deal with airports, baggage, traffic, and weather, not to mention the moods of members of his entourage less disciplined than himself. Marcel's life was a petri dish of predictability to the degree that he could control it, but of course, life refuses to be controlled, and it dishes out its own surprises.

I had never before experienced someone of such discipline or public exposure. I was a loose cannon by comparison. At home on my farm, I lived without clocks, mirrors, entourage, admirers, or curtain calls. Day was day and I worked. Night was night and I slept. My life was in keeping with the sun, moon, and weather. Nothing about me was of public interest. I could move freely about without hounding by paparazzi or autograph seekers. My feelings weren't hurt if no one recognized me on the street. If I received one personal letter a month, it was a major event. Twilight meant feeding time, not show time. If people came to visit, it was grounds for celebration, not reason to ask, "What do they want from me?" In this respect, our lives were worlds apart.

Given the all-consuming enormity of Marcel's life, I was deeply touched that he made time for me in it, and I, in turn, did my best to become a night person to accommodate him.

My initial tryst with Marcel was just a week, but the intensity of it made it seem like an eternity. As someone said about aging, "Praise the splendor, not the years." Often enough in those first few days, I wanted to bolt, to return to the comfort zone of my own pace, rhythms, simplicity—my own little life. I longed for the natural orbiting of day and night, without hype, spotlights, applause. But something compelled me to stay, to tough out the discomfort of living under his x-ray vision; I recognized that I was in the presence of a great master who was much more than the man himself. I saw him as an avatar of mime and a prophet of the human condition. To spend time in his presence was to experience the vast stillness of his field of perception. He was presence personified. The lessons I gained in that short time impacted me for a lifetime. Praise the splendor!

Marcel was obviously no stranger to panic attacks. They seemed to heighten his scrutiny. His sense of observation was his currency, and it was all part of his process to make every emotion serve as grist for his mime mill, to integrate into the immense archive of material for his show. Even my moments of desperation to escape his scrutiny became a subject of fascination for him. The more uncomfortable I became, the more he seemed to study the details of emotions playing out before him. He studied my every expression and gesture, even my breathing, as though it was all being crafted into a skit for his show. I was on the hot seat all the time. In fact, I felt like I was all the women rolled into one in his skit "The Dating Service," where the coat buttons never quite match up and are always one off; where the hired date is too tall, short, aggressive, klutzy, or demure; where someone's foot is always being stepped on; where the perpetrator of desire ends up being the servant to that desire; where the effort to get it right is trying too hard.

The illusive "it" to get it right, to please the impossible master, was exhausting. I was suffering from an overdose of his X-ray vision, and my own repetitive mantra: "Watch what you wish for." Pushed to my limit, I finally became grounded enough to shed any pretense of who I wished I was and become absolutely real with him, accepting us both completely for who we were and were not. I met him face to face. When he studied me, I studied him right back. We read each other.

Perceiving my struggle, he said, "It takes tremendous emotional stability to live life without illusion."

Once I gave up trying to please him, we entered a new comfort level with each other. We resonated on the same frequency. We neither pushed or shoved the other. I came to understand how seemingly mismatched couples could bond. The realness was the glue, not the buzz or the appearance of right or wrong.

I found Marcel infinitely fascinating, a marvelous raconteur. His childlike curiosity and playfulness were captivating. He had the ability to turn any moment into the ridiculous or the macabre. Life with Marcel was alive, filled with a quixotic spirit that constantly changed. Nothing was commonplace. Dimensions fanned out in all directions. He had the ability to enter inside the moment and bring it to life. Dinner at a restaurant became an improvised skit in which he animated objects on the table or manifested objects that didn't exist. His world was vast. I was enthralled. I soaked him in. Once I gave up the hopeless endeavor of trying to thread my ego through the eye of his needle, I was, indeed, hopelessly smitten. Was this the same man I had found so impossible just a few days before? Could change happen so fast? He became wondrous in my eyes.

He taught me to cast aside judgments and to plumb the source of energy of the other person. I learned to become the other person in my own body, to internalize his emotion, to inhabit it, to discover the point of focus—and then to stylize the gestures, to exaggerate ever so slightly the facial expressions, the weight of thought, the movements and nuances of the body. He taught me to breathe feeling into aliveness. He was teaching me the essence of mime. My hunger to learn from him was insatiable.

Marcel seemed captivated by me as well. I was a New Age renaissance woman. I was a free spirit and a risk-taker. I was a breath of fresh air to his life of schedules, repetition, predictability. We shared a European background, but I had broken free of the social template and was "out there" exploring new horizons. I had dared to do things that didn't, couldn't, enter the equation for him, but that his creative appetite hungered to experience, even if only vicariously.

We were both artists in the true sense of the word; ideas and conceptual visions were as real to us as anything concrete. We both possessed a craving for all that inspires the imagination, however outlandish. We were both subject to the quirky artistic temperament that can be a pain in the ass, understood only by another artist: hyper-sensitivity, sudden mood swings, and the need for acceptance. We were both romantics rooted in practicality. We respected each other's toughness and vulnerability.

Prior to meeting Marcel, I was of the mindset that men were attracted to women who were gorgeous, well-dressed, forever young, and seductive—head-turning trophies to flaunt and strut. Marcel seemed to be interested in me because of my boldness, courage, caring, emotional transparency, and nimble ability to adapt. He also recognized that we were a good fit. We shared a quiet harmony. And, oddly enough, he loved the way I dressed; it was always unpredictable and a little edgy. He saw in me the creative spark, and he honored me by soliciting my opinion and critique of his work. We brainstormed ideas for new skits. We shared the same ability to create form out of fantasy.

On the other hand, he was of the old world European culture, fine cut and polished to a high shine. I was an American-born gem in the rough. Once when I asked him about beauty, he responded, "La beauté ne se trouve pas dans la jeunesse; c'est dans l'ame; on as la visage qu'on merit." Beauty is not found in youth; it is in the soul; we have the face that we merit. (That said, I later noticed that he cherry-picked his women from an abundant pool of the young and beautiful. His third wife, for example, was his brother's son's girlfriend. She was twenty-three at the time. Marcel must have been in his sixties.)

Our time together became a blending of discovery of each other, of art, sketching each other, multilingual conversations, his performances every night, dinners with special friends and fans, and the precious time we shared afterward.

Because so much of Marcel's time was spent tending to business during the day, to keep me company, he delegated a playwright of my generation. Actually, I wondered if it was to keep me company or to spy on me and report back everything I said about him. Whatever the motivation, Mike and I became friends. He ended up as the liaison between Marcel and myself. He was the man in whose hands the power lay.

After dealing with the happenings of each day, when the voices of the world ceased to make demands on Marcel's time and attention, we rediscovered each other anew in our hotel suite.

"It's not the physical act of making love that is difficult at my age," he said. "It's finding the *desire* to make love." It was a strange thing for him to say, since he never seemed to lose that desire, not then, not ever.

In the comfort of his silence, he reached for me, and I lost myself in his embrace, in oneness with him. His ocean caressed my shore.

We were given the gift of each other, a gift in which time stood still.

Chapter 11
A Taste of the Divine

Clear morning light rimmed the drawn double curtains, brightening the edges of our hotel bedroom. I awoke before he did. Marcel was still in deep sleep beside me, breathing softly in the twilight zone of afterglow intermingled with deep fatigue. A smile crossed my lips remembering last night.

I propped myself up on one elbow to better take in the scene at hand. Our clothes were strewn all over the floor from undressing each other layer by layer on our way to the bed. After our first three painfully awkward days and nights on the world's longest blind date, we'd finally synchronized ourselves, and it was worth the wait. The sex improved dramatically. Our bodies were tuning to each other like two diverse instruments playing the same music. The subtle codes were no longer a mystery. I was adapting to his language of silence, and he seemed to be learning about my complex panel of erotic buttons and in what combinations to best engage them. We relinquished our precious egos for the tradeoff of greater union.

I felt it in the way he looked at me. The intensity of his gaze ranged from feather kisses on naked skin beneath my clothes in public to scorching temperatures well-placed to pulse my senses. I felt it in the resonance of his voice touching me like the chords of a cello, spreading throughout my entire being, a rush of warmth all the way to my abdomen, throbbing the recesses of my eros. I felt it in his touch, which he so masterfully employed as a channel for his massive energy. I lay beside him in utter wonderment.

He was a god onstage, filling theaters around the world with his power of presence. Its force could stop a train. He was well aware that his ability was also a shortcoming. His perception and caricature of all things added up to a hypersensitivity that had no "off" button and could lead to sensory overload offstage. And it often did—for me, anyway.

Yet here I was, lying next to him, and all I wanted to do was touch him again: to touch his body that had performed such miracles the night before when we were together. He was something else, all right. I wanted to frame his face in kisses, to pass my lips across his and slowly trace the tip of my tongue along the aperture of his mouth. I wanted to breathe him in, toy with his chest hairs with the tip of my nose while inhaling his musk. I wanted to nip at his nipples and flick them with my tongue. My fingers wanted to trace down along the sides of his torso, interplaying the touch with light kisses. I wanted to kiss his waist, and encircle his navel in kisses—that sacred center of the umbilical cord, the root of life's beginning, playing my tongue into its inner fold, then on down his abdomen and his god rod, now shielded in repose. I wanted to take it into my mouth, to savor it again before the day took its claim on him.

But I did none of those things, because he had a busy day of appointments ahead of him, plus another big performance that night, and he needed his sleep.

He stirred slightly and I held my breath; I didn't want him to wake up and shatter the spell I was in. He remained asleep, and I kept looking at him with wonderment and adoration.

To Marcel, sex was as diverse as his life, although without the same self-confidence. This was an arena that was close to his nerve line, as it was to mine, and probably everyone's. Though I was initially turned off by his androgyny, once I got beyond that, I came to love it. It doubled the excitement and the depth of perception. Marcel had a real feel for a woman: her vanities, vulnerabilities, sensitivities, sensibilities. After all, he knew all about the joy and dread of makeup and mirrors and having good and bad hair days (although in his case, that meant having his wig off-kilter like a mop). He knew about eyeliner and lipstick and moisturizers and "How do I look?" His x-ray vision, so relentless during my first few days with him, settled into the comfort of being seen and understood.

Just as I advanced in appreciation of the expressive language of mime, so too did I become adept in creating a silent language of sexual expression. I learned to perceive and decipher infinitesimal signals from him. I learned to excite subtle sensations in his erogenous zones as surely as he played the music of mine. Our melded imaginations manifested in the poetry of movement: we became as gentle breezes caressing fields of swaying grass, barely touching flesh as our hands passed over the delicate body hair.

Marcel had the ability to project any part of himself into any part of me, so I experienced my body as a myriad of G-spots. For example, all he had to do was slide his arm up my spine and it felt like one long electric rush of energy that was an arrow into my thrill zone. He also had the power to levitate my whole body with his tongue. That tongue! It was a flame that elevated me to paroxysms of pure rapture.

I tried to do the same to him with mine. I traced my tongue from his brain stem to his coccyx. I took his penis into my mouth until it vanished into pure pleasure. With my tongue, I flicked its tip, circled along its trunk, and drew it in deeper and deeper. He loved to watch it vanish into me.

Sex with Marcel became a wonderland with no end in sight. We became as storms at sea, rolling, heaving, and thrusting ourselves in and out of each other, with waves of passion that didn't quite crest, but continued to mount higher and higher.

I wondered if he was like this with all his lovers, or if it was a quality unique to us. My thoughts of Marcel were always accompanied by images of other women. And yet, he had the ability to make me feel absolutely special to him, just as I did that first night in the theater surrounded by hundreds of other people. He had that gift.

I couldn't imagine life without him. Without his touch, his all-engulfing force, and his depth of soul, life was a dimmer switch on the lowest light, a mere pilot light in a sea of gray.

The final night of our week-long blind date together came all too soon. The last night of his Detroit show marked the end of his

American tour. The applause had subsided. The chatter of dinner was behind us. We returned to our hotel room arm-in-arm, as if for the first time, as if it had always been this way and always would be. The shoe fit and I wasn't ready for our time together to end. I didn't want to return to my life as a scullery maid and field worker with my best music still unsung, so I went all out. I bypassed my monkey mind envisioning other women and no tomorrows and gave myself totally to being with Marcel, now. I took him in without fear or doubt.

An expansive silence surrounded us. We stood there observing each other from head to toe, inch by inch. Not as sex objects, not as god or goddess, not as give or get, not as trophies, but as the two wondrous imperfect people that we were. The unmitigated scrutiny of the artist in us both took in every detail, not for the sake of judgment, but just to imprint the impression upon the blank canvass of the mind. Then, as if responding from the mutual impulse of one mind, we reached for each other in an embrace that was absolute and complete. We were engulfed. I could feel the enormity of his presence, his embracing heart, his rising desire, his tenderness mounting into passion. I followed his lead, in perfect harmony with him, his fire fueling mine, mine fueling his, rising in heat and intensity, ablaze, fused, roaring! Our clothes fell easily away until we stood naked. No words were needed. We were of one mind and total acceptance.

This gracious suite of rooms filled with flowers reduced itself to just us, nothing more. Marcel flipped the switch of just one light, turning the room into a twilight zone, then kissed me in a way that was neither lust-filled nor lackluster, but rather a statement of deep-felt desire: desire based on a longing that transcended time itself. His longing for true bonding resonated with my own, and I responded in kind. I opened to him completely. We knew each other's body by now, yet never before like this. His magical hands were as a bow on the strings of my violin. We were in perfect sync, true accord, in absolute understanding and openness. This was the dance I wanted from him, the otherworldly experience I sensed was possible; this was the true connection we had glimpsed but never dared to own. This, this, was why I came. This was the chalice I had quested for all my life. This was the source from which all else springs.

And still we kept going, fused in body, mind and soul in the unspoken commitment to the moment, without interruption, free of fear, in total attention to the miracle of our togetherness. It felt as though my synapses could bear no more intensity. I could no longer distinguish the boundaries of our bodies, of who was who, of where the one began and the other ended. A powerful force was rising fast and hot, rising, rising ever higher, soaring upward on a beam of white light, breaking through the darkness all around. The force of the light drew us ever upward, ever higher, until it arrived at its source: Marcel in whiteface!

This enormous wave of energy crested in a crescendo of cascading light that spilled forth from the inside out, as Marcel emptied himself into me, then crashed onto the shore of my heaving breasts.

Nothing in my life had ever equaled it. It was transformative. It filled me completely.

When my senses gently re-entered my body, I opened my eyes to look at Marcel lying there beside me. His face was beatific. It had lost all its tension and he appeared as a young man in his prime. I couldn't stop marveling at him.

"I love you." I whispered directly in his ear.

Was his silence a sacrament to the moment or—something else? He smiled a gentle smile, held me close, and we drifted off to earthly sleep in the cradle of our bodies breathing as one.

The seas of our separateness, which had parted to give us this passage of togetherness, now closed over once again. By dawn we were two individual swells in an ocean of many currents.

The next day, I felt something was askew. We had never spoken of his other women, but their existence was apparent. Unable to contain myself any longer and needing a reality check, I asked Marcel if he had other lovers at present.

Yes, he said, he had special friends in other places.

Then I dared to do something I'd never done before. I exposed my vulnerability to him in broad daylight and I asked him if he loved me.

Marcel, now completely composed and reborn from our extraordinary night, drew himself up, flicked his two middle fingers up and down as though to downsize the immensity of the question, and calmly replied, *"À ma manière"* (In my style").

That wasn't the response I wanted to hear. I was suddenly a woman alone, midway out on a tightrope, spanning a fearsome void. One end of the wire was battened down on the high platform of departure, but the other end of the wire was only clenched tightly in my teeth.

The drive to the airport was a solemn journey of distancing. As he held me in a final embrace, I experienced the rending apart of what had been for me the greatest oneness I had ever known.

He enfolded me in his deep embrace, saying, "The language of the heart cannot lie, for in order to lie, you must have the words."

I was overcome with emotion. Was the salt I tasted in our kiss from his tears or mine?

His parting words to me were, "I'll call you."

Chapter 12
The Ravages of Silence

I waited for that call like a dog waits in the road for the return of its beloved master, the object of its devotion, with ears cocked in all directions straining for the slightest indication.

I waited and waited and waited for that call.

My hope waited, my expectation waited, my outreached love waited, my longing waited.

Every cell in my body waited, through every minute and every breath and every heartbeat of every day. Then every week. And on into more than a month.

I waited with joyous expectancy, then bafflement, then hurt, then anger, then rage.

The voice of silence turned vicious, stalking me with cliché visions of unrequited love and images of lovers who had been used and discarded as nonchalantly as a Dixie cup.

I had just come through a divorce; I was still emotionally raw from the dissolution of my relationship with Dennis. I had not survived that painful ordeal to enter another at the hands of the master of perception. No! A large and furious beast of self-righteous indignation was coming to life and sounding its fearsome roar: "Never again!"

Apoplexy surged through my veins. Marcel was on tour, but he was *always* on tour. That was no excuse. He was performing in urban theaters, staying in fine hotels in major cities, not in a tent in some deep dark jungle of the Mesozoic Age. There were telephones. There was mail service.

How could he be so heartless? Was I just the butterfly in his skit "The Butterfly Catcher," wherein the hapless Bip pursues a lovely butterfly that, after a good chase hither and yon, he catches in his net, then coarsely manhandles, causing its desperate fluttering death in his own hand? Was that what was happening here? Court, capture, and kill?

"Oh Marcel! Don't you realize that matters of the heart are fragile and mortal? Love needs nurturing, the chalice needs tending, for its nectar is life's only true source. Love is not a one-man show, it's a sharing and a caring, involving two people. The channels of communication must be kept open and clear, for fantasy is filled with intruders eager to maraud and destroy. Oh Marcel! Never take love for granted. It hates to wait and withers from weariness or self-destructs from abandonment. Nothing is so good that it cannot turn horrid."

Days darkened into more dark days.

His silence became a form of nihilism to me. Images filled my mind: was life to him really just theatrics? Had he been play-acting with me all along? Was his gut-wrenching intensity and "language of the heart" just a sham? Was he really like every other man I had ever known: just interested in getting laid? Was our miraculous connection and transcendental sex merely grist for his next act? Was our pioneering of uncharted realms of emotional surrender just a diversion from his grinding schedule? How was it possible to withdraw to such a degree—to remain out of touch for such an insufferable period of time?

I wondered if Marcel had been struck by a lightning bolt from the heavenly command tower, reminding him that he was indeed sent to earth to fulfill a purpose, and that carousing for real was not part of the celestial plan. I felt like such a common mortal in this scheme of things.

I felt his absence everywhere. The sky no longer brimmed with promise. There was a fearful vacancy in my heart. My feelings, so flowing over with joyous love for him, became a mockery of themselves. How quickly joy and happiness had twisted into demons of darkness that hacked and tore at my every thought. All that was filled with the warmth of promise became a wasteland, now charred and broken.

This fall from Grace transported me to the Underworld where every image was dark. I envisioned a scene from World War II: a desperate refugee walking like a ghost through the ash-covered ruins of her once-beautiful city.

I felt like one among many in the Underworld's Lake of the Damned, reaching out from a sense of loss, hoping for a call, waiting for a letter, craving an outstretched hand to grasp onto and be saved at last from drowning in disillusion.

Under that whiteface, was he just a cold-blooded vampire in disguise, who sucked the life-force from his women?

I hated the way I felt, and even more, I hated him for eliciting such feelings, then trashing them. What on earth was he thinking as he hid behind his silent wall for more than a month now, leaving me severed from our powerful connection?

Or was it that he wasn't thinking? Was it that he was involved in other things, with other people—with maybe, possibly, probably other lovers in other ports!

How stupid and naive and puny I felt to assume that because our connection meant the world to me, it would have impacted him in the same way. In my misery, I had forgotten that Marcel was the master of illusion. He courted it. He toyed with it. He had conquered its energy.

In moments of clarity, I questioned: If it's all just an illusion, what had I really lost? I realized I felt the loss of the buoyancy and expansiveness that this illusion brought, the being in love with illusion, without which my life seemed clay-footed. I had lost that grandiose feeling of loving, and being loved by the wondrous Marcel Marceau, the dark side of which was feeling bitch-slapped by silence.

Would that I had a grasp of the bigger picture: that he was incapable of the kind of relationship I wanted, so I needed to realize that something wasn't there on a personal level, because this world-renowned deity was operating on another level entirely. He wasn't available in that way. That's why he created Bip, as a receptacle for the feelings he didn't want to own. It probably all stemmed from the war: Marcel had recovered creatively from the trauma of those years, but he hadn't recovered in terms of his human relationships.

Bolstered by weeks and weeks of introspection and brutal honesty, I gave myself one last chance to back out of the radical measure I'd determined to take. I turned back the pages, and this time I read the writing on the wall. First but not least, I recalled that he didn't respond when I said, "I love you."

There were, of course, other signs and indications that I never fully allowed myself to recognize, let alone accept. They flew in the face of my fantasy. How many times do you have to get run over to learn to recognize road kill?

Finally, I could no longer withstand the river of pain. It took a large amount of fury-fuel, but I managed to propel myself out of his orbit. Oh hindsight of a thousand eyes: give me your vision. And the vision was, anyone who lives with her head in the clouds does so with her heart on the chopping block.

So I did what I had to do to take charge of myself. I drove the cold stake of determination into my heart. Then I turned my back and I moved on. But not in silence. Oh no! Insult is always a cheap shot, but it is an arrow in the quiver of anger. I took out my pen and used it as a weapon.

I knew Marcel hated the word "fuck." It offended his sensibilities. It implied banality, triviality. It tweaked a nerve. It reminded him of his family's gritty station in life, from which he had struggled long and hard to better himself. It smacked of "bourgeois," a French word that carries social disdain.

It also reminded him of his first love.

As is often the case with virgins in Europe, his first sexual experience was with an older working woman, a baker, as I recall. His idealistic spirit romanticized her into his Eve, the most wondrous creature on Earth in the garden of earthly delights. The bubble popped before it became airborne; they weren't cut of the same cloth. They both came from working-class backgrounds, but Marcel's gift was something special and he knew it. To her, however, he was just another guy, just another "mec," just another fuck. Her coarse abasement of him imprinted deep.

sketch by Paulette Frankl

Marcel! How dare you treat me this way!

Now I felt I, too, was being demeaned as just another fuck by the most wondrous of men. The demons he'd unleashed in me took hold of my hand and wrote out the crude word he hated most, using it as a weapon against him.

"How dare you treat me like this, you fucker!"

Chapter 13
Aftermath of the Storm

I had thrown myself away, wholeheartedly it turned out, to experience as much of Marcel as possible in our short eternity together. Now I experienced the loss of myself as well as of him.

"Silence frightens people sometimes," Marcel later told me. "We have to enter inside silence to discover it's not solitude, it's solidarity." Later, much later, I drew comfort from those words. But during that epic bout with silence, all I could think of was I felt so alone, so lost and abandoned in the vastness of his deafening silence. It felt like a cruel cop-out.

Searching for survivor skills from Bip, I was reminded of the skit "Bip Commits Suicide." The ever-bungling Bip, always a loser at love, is heartbroken over his unrequited love with a woman. Consumed with self-pity and grief, he decides to take the "romantic" way out: suicide. He looks at the photo of his beloved one last time, then at his own sad image in the mirror. Passing his hand over her photo in a final gesture of farewell, Bip places his battered hat with the drooping flower on the floor, then picks up a pistol to finish off the job. But Bip the bungler can't even pull off his own suicide. His hand shakes uncontrollably. He can't remember the location of his heart: is it on the right or left side of his chest? He can't make his hand obey his mind. It holds the gun too high, or too low, so he points it at his head instead. But before he can get the aim straight, the pistol goes off accidentally, nearly scaring him to death, which catapults him into a different frame of mind altogether. Having come so close to death, Bip reconsiders life. He revisits the photo of his love and concludes maybe things aren't so bad after all. The piece ends with him clutching the photo to his heart and spinning in circles of joy. How quickly Marcel was able to turn joy to sorrow and back again onstage. If only matters of the heart resolved themselves that quickly in real life.

*sketches by
Marcel Marceau*

Word got back to me via a letter from Mike, the playwright spy, that Marcel was terrified I was trying to *possess* him.

"*Possess* him? Is he out of his blithering mind?"

Obviously, his sense of illusion was suffering from what I call SPD: Severe Projection Disorder.

"*He's* the control freak, not me! Sure, the sex had achieved oneness, but that's not the same as friggin' spell-casting *possession*!"

This accusation only made matters worse.

Anais Nin writes: "She wept because they were so close in that earthy darkness, close in the magnetic pull between their skin, their hair, their bodies, and yet their dreams never touched at any point, their vision of life, their attitudes. She wept over the many dislocations of life, forbidding the absolute unity."

When the gods are bored, they amuse themselves by watching us mortals writhe. The gods are cruel voyeurs who entertain themselves by pulling aside the curtain in the chamber of lovers, just far enough to see, but not be seen. They watch, with bulging eyes all over their faces, the lascivious acts that unfold before them, and take their pleasure vicariously.

They view the moves and hear the moans, know the salty tastes and sense the pressure of skin on skin. They well understand the heat of desire, recognize the crest of climax, and can almost feel the rush of release, the ahhhhhhh of it all.

The gods giveth and the gods taketh away. They respond to our prayers, they participate in our pleasures, and then they steal them away from us like thieves—because they can. However, they also leave behind a token, a souvenir, a bit of wisdom, if we're alert enough to recognize it. The insight I received from my time with Marcel was that the experience was a gift! It wasn't a promise of ever-after. It wasn't even a guarantee of ever again. It was simply a moment in which two strangers overcame the demons of ego and insecurity and, yes, expectation to find common ground, to surrender and trust and experience, however fleeting, a taste of the divine.

As it turned out, the gods had more twisted mischief to set forth. My letter calling Marcel a fucker crossed in the mail with his.

The long-awaited word from Marcel began, "My dearest Paulette, you are the only person who understands my need for silence!"

Oh NO!

His letter was filled with praise, love, and desire! Now he was reaching out to *me*, but it was too late. Little did he know I had just hurled him a volcano! It spewed boulders and lava and my fury fire all over him. The result was catastrophic. But I was helpless to do anything about it. There was no turning back. The gods are capricious. They make no guarantees as to forgiveness.

In his follow-up letter, he was so upset, I couldn't read his handwriting. I'll never know what he said. Then all communication ceased.

It took me over a year to untangle and reclaim my feelings, to regain my equilibrium and sense of self.

The waves of time lapped the shore, scouring clean the egregious wounds we'd each suffered from the other. Both the hallelujah and the damnation of our encounter subsided. Life on the farm returned to birdsong in the apple trees. The seasons changed with their sowings and harvests.

Marcel remarried for the third time.

The world turns. The painted ponies go up and down. We're captive on the carousel of time. The show always goes on.

Chapter 14
Lessons in Silence

The show goes on with its endless changes in time and space, but the silence remains the same—spaceless, timeless, changeless. After all, what's the natural state of a theater? What's left when the applause ends and the audience goes home? Silent emptiness. Silence is the language of eternity.

And that was the deeper lesson that the gods left me: as the silence of mime fills a theater, as the silence of trees holds an orchard, so the silence of consciousness occupies the universe. Only in silence do we encounter our true Self.

The "show," the grand illusion of names and shapes imposed on the world by minds and egos, the endless parade of transient actions, experiences, and events driven by desire and fear, these are merely waves on the surface of the boundless, fathomless ocean. And the entertainment of movies, music, museums, amusements, mime, and the like? Shows within the show, reflections of the mirror of the mind.

Yet that was Marcel Marceau's world, and I learned that I'd simultaneously idealized and minimized it.

In one of my desperate attempts at connection, I had the audacity to write to him, "You could be so much more than a name on a dressing room door and a vase of dead flowers."

Since I perceived him as god-like on stage, I fancied he could also be a true leader of our troubled world. His language of the heart could be prophetic. As my personal pain diminished, I came to a clarity of realization about the deeper lesson: Marcel, especially through Bip, was expressing a profound universal message: that of the interconnectedness of all beings. That in spite of the diversities of cultures and differences of language, we all shared the same understanding and response of core emotions.

Another thing—Marcel made it clear to me that *I* was the one who didn't understand: his life *was* the theater and it would never be otherwise. To Marcel, the theater was his second chance at life: to recreate life, on his own terms, according to the idealism of his pre-Nazi youth. He could control the components and endings in his mimodrames and pantomimes.

Later, I read a supporting statement in an interview with Valerie Bocheck in her book *Le Mime Marcel Marceau.*

"I can construct a world as I would like it to be, presenting the heartbreaking destruction, the malevolence, but not ending with the abandonment, but with a cry of hope. I believe in human redemption through theatre."

"The Third Eye" is a poem Marcel wrote in 1981.

> The torrents of our life flow drop by drop …
> My fist bleeds through too much battering …
> Oh! Incessant combats of humanity,
> Discoveries, blessings, griefs, cries of love and hate,
> Thirst for liberty, you are but thoughts that brave
>   becoming …
> Where are you humankind who dream of love eyes open
>   in the light?
> A While ago the angel smiled at the wing-torn devil
>   halting in his flight, his laughter not Homeric as he
>   hoped, for conscience shattered it.
> My soul has hugged a secret just as yours, that of
>   tomorrow in an intangible world.
> Lands of the future, flamboyant suns,
> Stars of sapphire,
> There will be more bright battles where the cries and
>   tears are those of love emerging from the shades …
> All things converge in vast creative thought.
> Now enter the new age.

> The sovereign spirit is in the firmament of stars.
> Being is lit …
> Love and liberty hold out their arms to us.
> My dream, assure me that the third eye is.
> I more than need the time to love and live …
> Time is the great healer.
> Too quick the question nags: where is the third eye, where?
> The near forgotten angel brushed my shoulder with his wing …
> One thing I ask: know that we always bear this third eye deep within our inmost selves.

Finally, the great mime Jean-Louis Barrault wrote the following in his book *Souvenirs Pour Demain,* regarding his own marriage to the theater, I raised the curtain as one does some forbidden thing. I took a few paces on the stage where, not long before, I had been so frightened. I stood for a moment motionless at the edge of the stage. The Silence of the theatre came over me. I was caught in it as though in ice. There was frost all round me and on me. I was soon covered over with a hoarfrost of Silence. … Now my childhood dream had come true: I was living, was at that very moment marrying the life of the theatre. I came to realize in the course of that night of initiation that the whole problem of the theatre is to set that Silence vibrating. Unfreeze the Silence. Move upstream. When a river flows into the sea, it dies; its estuary is its deathbed. What has to be done is to go upstream, to get to the source, to birth, to essence."

CHAPTER 15

The Counsel of Hindsight

The radical plunge from ecstasy to agony to acceptance to realization resulting from my union with Marcel shook loose a lot of issues in my psyche regarding love, abandonment, and despair. They needed processing. It took time.

If I could converse now with that proud, idealistic, headstrong young woman in the prime of her life, from the standpoint of who I am today, I would hold her close to my heart, stroke her troubled head, and gently say to her: Understanding does not come easily. The secrets of realization are revealed through the pain of experience, your own decoding of his silence. You locked onto the old cliché of victim/blame and you ran with it.

I would say to her: It was no accident that you and Marcel were drawn to each other. You each had something to give to and teach the other. You needed his detachment and depth to move forward in your life. He needed your daring and abandon in order to evolve in his life.

He never made any promises to you. He gave you all that he had to offer: his presence, good, bad, and indifferent. Once you experienced that, you wanted more. You wanted relationship. But even if you'd gotten your way, you would have lived your life in his shadow. Other people's shadows are not designed for two and have a way of growing too small too fast. He had no room in his life for the kind of partnership you wanted. He did, however, give you the greatest gift of acknowledging you as a kindred creative spirit. It was your work to make the most of that validation.

We are initially drawn to people because we identify with common qualities, recognize our own experience in them. The miracle of Marcel was that he was able to ignite and awaken that recognition in his audiences the world over. Everyone could identify with the emotions—hopes, fears, struggles, desires, despair, humor—he evoked. Because he was in perfect alignment with himself when he was onstage, they experienced the feeling of that alignment within themselves, which in turn led to a sensation of ascension. Because he was vibrating on *all* levels, body, mind, and spirit, his beholders couldn't help resonate with him on some level. It was a contact high. That's why he was an icon. That was his power. That's what you experienced with him: that transference of wholeness and of ascendance. You tuned yourself to him. For *you*, it was the ultimate awakening. For him, it was just who he was.

You experienced perfect harmony with him, and in that long spell of his silence, you felt cleaved apart, expelled, disconnected from your bond with him. Now you were left to deal with the morbid matter of your own disharmony, your own imbalance. You reacted. You fell back on social programming: you were insulted, enraged, righteously indignant, standing up for violated rights. You resorted to exactly what you accused him of doing: thinking of only yourself. But the fact is, you needed to do that. You couldn't have reclaimed your life without breaking your bond with him. You needed to find and fortify that strength within yourself. That wasn't a bad thing in and of itself; it was the way you did it that was unfortunate. It caused repercussions that took a long time to heal.

You had just come through a divorce and an abortion. You longed for wholeness, for union. He had just come through a second divorce. He no doubt longed for a good fling with no strings attached. He was flexible with his body, but guarded and withholding of his emotions. Silence was the perfect trap door through which to seek escape. Silence! The universal language and the universal enigma.

Neither of you was so highly evolved in the expertise of relationships that you could withstand the storm on the surface by abiding in the peace and love found in the depths. That calls for detachment and acceptance, for allowing the other his own experience of the storm without reacting, without rocking the boat of togetherness. That's a tough one: hanging in there because you value your togetherness more than your need to be right.

Marcel was a great master on stage, and his message was the language of the heart. But offstage, he wasn't so skilled at dealing with those same matters. Artists can be incredibly evolved in one narrow realm and quite *un*evolved in others. With acceptance comes compassion, for the times that he wasn't grand, when he fell short, when he was scared, needy, or absent. On the stage, he was presence personified. But in the messy complexities of relationships, in real life, he bumbled along, tripping and falling, rising and dusting himself off, just like the rest of us. He was Bip, always aspiring to the greatness that eluded him, and settling instead for humble joys, the outcome of hard knocks.

Don't forget, I would remind her, that Marcel's mentality was forged in fear. His war years brought him face to face with imprisonment and annihilation. His fear of entrapment was what he projected onto you. Then there were his fears of alienation, inadequacy, not measuring at the top, where the only place to go is down. At the same time, he felt chosen, and innately superior. It's amazing that he could live under those kinds of pressures.

One could safely say that mime saved his life. It grounded him and gave him a channel of expression for all these powerful emotions. He survived by distancing himself from them, by studying, scrutinizing, and reenacting them. He crafted Bip to do the job of guiding him into and through overwhelming experiences by use of emotional caricature.

I would remind her that Marcel was a man of great courage. That he invited you to join him on a blind date spoke volumes about him, and about you for accepting. Who does either? You walked out on that tightrope together, stepping off your own platforms in life. This was especially impressive in light of the fact that Marcel wasn't one to embrace surprises.

Though you initially couldn't help playing the blame card, it was a great turning point for you to reclaim your power. You hoped he'd throw you a lifeline, but in fact you took claim to the greatest lifeline of all: your own. You moved on. The spell was broken.

It had to be. Although he tried to do both, the demands of domesticity didn't fit the realities of his profession. It was his choice and his great sacrifice.

I would, in the end, have her recall the image of him miming the crucifixion, his arms outstretched, his head limp on his shoulder, the heat of the stage lights causing his eye makeup to streak down his prominent cheek bones, appearing like a trail of black tears on a white skull. It was the perfect metaphor of the sacrifice he made for his immortality.

Marcel was who he was. So were you. The way you were together, and apart, was exactly how it was meant to be.

Chapter 16
Booty Call

Two years later, in 1974, the phone rang. It was Marcel. He was in San Francisco for a blitz trip. Could we meet for breakfast at seven a.m. before his flight out?

I agreed, and arranged to spend the night prior to our rendezvous at my friend Kimi Dios' apartment, just blocks away from Marcel's hotel, so I wouldn't have to drive from the farm to San Francisco in the wee hours.

While I was excited to see him, I was also wary. It would be our first one-on-one time since the big blowout. He was obviously playing it safe by inviting me to breakfast in a public place.

Wanting to look my best for our brief rendezvous, before going to sleep that night I drenched my long hair in Kimi's Tahitian coconut oil, an old Polynesian beauty secret. I made sure to set the alarm in plenty of time to wash and dry my hair before breakfast, thus appearing with hair in gleaming glory.

At two-thirty in the morning, the phone rang, awakening the household. It was Marcel, eager to meet and not wanting to wait until breakfast. "*Viens vite!*" Come at once! His voice was filled with excitement.

Good god! I was thrilled that he couldn't wait. I loved his spontaneity and I was excited to see him too. At the same time, I was in no way ready to rush over to his hotel for a booty call. I didn't have the hour it would take just to shower and wash out that coconut oil, which, when not enveloped in the warmth of the tropics, stiffens and smells funny. Anyway, we weren't on the kind of terms required to explain my dilemma. I felt a modicum of mystique was always good to maintain. After all, he never took off his wig when he was with me, and I had no desire to look like Medusa, with long ropes of stiffened snakes in rancid coconut oil when I was with him.

What to do? Grab hold of the moment, let the vanities be damned and go be with Marcel for the precious little time we had together? Or meet him as planned for breakfast, feeling rested, showered, composed, and looking presentable?

I figured, we're both artists, and artists look life in the face. He should be able to take it that he gets what he calls for at this ungodly hour, expecting me leap out of bed from a deep sleep to come at once. So I bit the bullet and went as is, coconut snakes and all.

I entered his room filled with trepidation. To add to my self-consciousness, a pimple from stress was festering right in the middle of my forehead. I dobbed it with goop, but that only seemed to irritate it. This was the litmus test. Could Marcel see beyond face value into unadorned essence? Or would he be repelled by seeing me like this, out of kilter with whatever illusion and expectation might be left over from two years before. Was I real to him or just a wet dream?

Marcel's expression was a combination of joy and shock, just as mine had been that first time we met in Chicago, when his bad breath dominated our rendezvous, sending waves of revulsion down my spine.

I noticed that his hotel room was vastly smaller than the ones in the past—an indication that box-office sales were not going so well and money was being pinched.

Veiling his thoughts behind his curtain of silence, Marcel overrode the moment with barely a "hello," then got right to the point: he unbuttoned his pants. No time to waste. The rosy rod was out and eager to get down to business. Bypassing conversation, Marcel was grabbing at my clothes.

"Doucement!" Slow down, I said, as I gently distanced myself to adjust to what my fantasies had thought our get-together would be: a nice chatty catch-up visit and a much needed heart to heart, together with some affectionate moments to rekindle our closeness. After all, *his* life might have been all about silence, but mine was all about communication, staying in touch, remaining present one way or another, keeping the energy alive. We weren't on the same wavelength at all regarding time and how it stretches and contracts and twists and distorts. It had been at least a year with no letter, card, call, or word from him, following the year of our emotional collision. Silence has a way of freezing memory in place. I wasn't about to take up where we'd left off in 1972 and filet my body and soul to feed his fleeting lust.

I was caught in that place most women know: to succumb or not to succumb? If the answer is negative, then the shut-down process is automatic. And once set in motion, it's not an easy thing to reverse.

My mind went into emergency overdrive. "OK," I thought. "I'll play along. But on *my* terms."

He obviously didn't realize that our miraculous sex back then was because I'd opened and given myself to him completely. In no way did I hold back; I was in love with him and I wanted that sacred union with him. He obviously didn't get that transcendent sex is profound, a bonding and a blending. Marcel Marceau was in my cell structure, probably encoded in my DNA. However, after that trial-by-fire ordeal of disconnect by silence, followed by his proclamation that the theater was his *true* relationship, his true love and it would never be any other way—why would I want an encore of *that*?

On the other hand, here we were. There are many forms of turn-on. I fell back on my old standby, illusion, and turned lust into a peekaboo of the self-pleasure variety. He could be *my* audience for a change.

I did what Marcel does onstage with his audience every night: I envisioned a melding of our minds, so that my thoughts freely projected onto his. I stood there before him, looking right into him, as he so often did with me. I mentally pulled aside his veil of silence, just as he'd unveiled me, leaving me quivering in bare discomfort before his squint-eyed assessment.

I now observed *his* nakedness of thought, his discomfort at seeing me so out of alignment with his fantasy. Worse yet, the Medusa illusion ignited his worst fear—that women have the power to turn man's desire to stone.

Everything about him was shrinking before my eyes.

I saw that he didn't have the great emotional strength required to face life without illusion. And in that split second, I realized that the only reason I was standing in this room at all was because I'd written him that letter from the orchard, filled with more fantasy than any of his other fan mail. I represented to him one of the queens of fantasy. I saw that Marcel's world of illusion *was* his reality. He might be the great master of it, but it was also the master of him. Thus, it was OK for him to get ugly, but it was not okay for me to appear in front of him unappealingly, which was, after all, out of context with his fantasy.

Now the veils were removed, the truth revealed. His fantasy of me did not include this ruptured image that was off-turning. And I realized that Marcel bypassed foreplay because for him—perhaps for all narcissists—appearance *is* the foreplay. If the appearance passes approval, nothing more is needed.

Here I stood. I had come to him as summoned, but not as he'd imagined. I was now the object of his "nots"—just as he had been the object of my "if onlys": I was not the embodiment of his fantasy, I was not fulfilling his illusion, I was not as he'd remembered or desired. He did not want the real me in real time. Not at all. And this fear thing was a cold knife in his blood that struck panic to his groin.

After all the hoops I'd jumped through to please him in the past and the painful process to learn to live without him, to detach myself from him, I now felt my own strength in my core, unashamed of who I was before the eyes of the master, who was clearly diminishing in size before me.

Once again, I thought of his skit "The Dating Service," which is supposed to provide Bip with the perfect woman. A number of women ring his doorbell. The first is too tall; she overpowers him, making him feel small, inadequate. The next is too fat; he fears being smothered by her folds of flesh. The next is too aggressive; he retreats from her rapacious hunger. The last, whom he observes out the window, is just right, but by now Bip has become so afraid of the sound of the doorbell ringing, so afraid of his own disappointment, his need for perfection, that he hesitates too long; the sounding doorbell rings too many times, goes unanswered for too long, and the moment is lost, never to be retrieved.

Ahhhhh Marcel, if you look life in the face, you will note that in the theater of the absurd, everyone is actor, audience, and stage. Nothing and no one is static. Look! Look, Marcel! These Medusa vipers? These snakes growing from my scalp? They're just dreads, stiff with coconut oil. I wanted to be beautiful for you at breakfast! I wanted to maintain your illusion of me. I tried. But it wasn't to be.

I needed to break the spell.

Come with me, Marcel, into this journey of the transformation of fear into intrigue and intrigue into the awe of essence!

I took a dreadlock and passed it along my cheek like a finger of a caress; I touched it with my tongue, which was neither long and narrow nor forked at the tip. Then I placed both hands on my temples, as he did in his skit "The Mask Maker," but instead of being stuck behind a laughing mask, I was stuck behind the mask of ugliness, beneath which was the anguish of wanting to be seen as beautiful and desirable. I transformed my self-consciousness into the love and desire for him that had been buried alive by my shame; it arose within me and melted away all that was unsightly and threatening. I removed the mask and replaced it with a smile filled with warmth and—yes—desire, as I proceeded to remove my clothes, slowly, one button, one hook, one zipper at a time.

Holding Marcel in my gaze, I mimed for him erotica, swaying to my internal rhythms of eros. I acted out a cat-like dance of rubbing our bodies together, tracing my hand the length of his arm, then gripping his hand, while bracing my legs against his and dipping my naked body into a backward arch, my head thrown back in arousal. I rolled my shoulders in counter moves and rocked my hips in figure-eights, undulating my torso in the "S" curves of a belly dancer—holding Marcel in my focus as the object of my desire, just out of reach. I traced my fingertips up my extended leg, lightly touching the flesh along my inner thigh, lips apart and eyes closed, exploring the valley of my groin, cupping my mound of Venus in my palm, probing with my fingers into the frills and folds of its chambers. My fingers circled the erotic bead of my happy zone. I gasped in pleasure as I felt the thrill rise upward.

Marcel reached for me.

I took his hand in mine, turned it up, and touched my tongue to the base of his palm and wrist. My tongue flicked back and forth on that pleasure point before it licked upward along the lifeline and came to the crotch of his index and middle finger. There it played along the short ridge of connecting skin before I took his middle finger into my mouth all the way to its hilt. I gently drew it in and out of my mouth, flicking its tip with my tongue, encircling its length around and around, drawing it deeper into my mouth with a pulsing suction, never taking my eyes off of his. I placed my hand atop his and moved it to gently squeeze my breast. I placed his thumb and index finger to rub the tip of my blushing nipple. I had him work it between his fingers just beyond the point of excitement, to the brink of pain, which engaged a light show in my head.

I quickly removed his hand and pulled back, out of his reach again.

But then I stood very close and ran my hands downward along the curvature of my torso, my waist, and my hips, sensually, lovingly. My thumbs rounded the corner of my hips, then traced the edges of my bush; one hand settled on my upper thigh, the other ventured into the mysterious depths of heaven and hell's underworld between my legs.

Marcel watched with rapt attention as I spread my legs. Probing fingers vanished inside the dark cavern. A tongue of fire flashed through my body, followed by a network of tingles that radiated from my G-spot down my legs into the soles of my feet and upward to my hardened nipples, into my molars, and my crown. My skin was moist, my cheeks flushed. My abdomen buckled. My index and middle finger circled my clit, round and round, working the pleasure spot with increasing pressure. Hot juice issued from within.

I dipped my finger into the nectar and licked my finger. The salty tangy taste met my tongue. Now the sensations were becoming stronger, tumbling one atop another and escalating in intensity, like a violin rising to higher and higher notes until the strings can take no more. With eyes closed, I felt a surge of pleasure course upward and inward, all-encompassing, my body responding with hard downward thrusts. Groans issued from an ancient place older than time. My breath quickened and became shallow, then stopped altogether so as not to halt the surge of sensation coursing through my body. My back arched, my thighs and buttocks tensed. I gasped for breath as my senses burst apart into a galaxy set aflame, bursting again and again. I could feel fluid between my legs with each burst. My body fell from the sky, onto my clothes on the floor. I was limp with joy all over, smiling, tingling, alive.

Marcel beheld me with an expression of awe.

I encircled him in the golden glow of my mind's eye and took him in my arms, transferring all the sexual energy I'd just generated. I passed it on to him through the connection of our hearts, for although I still didn't want to take him into my body, I did welcome him back into my soul.

Then I gathered my clothes and began to get dressed.

With a lingering kiss on his quivering lips, I took my exit from Marcel, leaving behind the souvenir of my red-lace thong panties on the floor, still fragrant with the sweet tobacco scent of a young woman's sex.

CHAPTER 17
Wake-Up Call

Snap! Two fingers break the trance.

The fantasy dissolves and disintegrates.

In short, none of that ever happened.

The reality was we were each caught up in the illusion of memory, each fantasizing the other to be other than who we were. Marcel no doubt fantasized the young nymph he depicted in his artwork, with whom he could float away beyond this earthly plane. I imagined an older, grounded man-god with whom I could be real and who would accept me as I was.

But the booty call and coconut oil were real enough, so the rest was a cautious attempt to deal with the disconnect resulting from our wounds of two years earlier, without ever mentioning what happened. Because Marcel pretended they didn't exist, I didn't feel right about opening that vein.

Still, we obviously both wanted to reconnect. For him that meant sex without emotion; for me, that meant eros without sex. I didn't want to be manipulated again. Marcel had maintained his emotional distance from me, and now I was holding him in my safe zone. He was still the object of my fantasy, but I had no intention of giving him access to the inner temple. One-way relationships don't work for me.

We spent a couple of hours like people do who haven't seen each other in ages, ships crossing in a vast sea in the light of dawn. We were all awkward and angular, out of kilter, two crustaceans moving sideways, guarded, hesitant, groping anew to find meaning beneath the shell of words.

I did manage to get naked.

Marcel was lying on the bed with his pants down to his knees.

I was on my knees astride his thighs. When I looked down I saw the rosy tip of his penis hiding amidst a fold of flesh.

"Talk to it," he said.

I thought to myself, "How about *you* talking to *me*!" Then I realized he thought that was easier than us talking to each other.

Whatever his intention, I was taken aback by his command. I had never been asked to do such a thing before. Oh, I'd experienced dirty-talk, but this was improv with the withered manhood of a superstar, and whatever the outcome, the resultant memories were for keeps. Even trying to imagine such an act created a self-conscious separation that cast me into a cerebral head lock. I sat frozen, burning with insecurity, shy, awkward, hoping for a miracle.

Should I introduce myself? What if the penis replied, "Paulette who?" like Marcel had responded once when I called him in London. Chances are, it wouldn't even remember my voice! I couldn't just launch into a dialogue with an appendage that was now two years estranged!

Was this another of Marcel's diversions to maintain control? Or did it signify that he'd lost control?

Whatever it was, it was all new to me.

What I did know was that his shriveled penis needed *something* to rouse its attention. A wisp of a smile crossed my face as I thought of the French saying, "It's easier to open your mouth than raise your arm." And what did he expect me to say? "Come my chou-chou. It's me, Paulette. Remember me?" Oh God! This was awful!

Perhaps worst of all, I didn't know whose penis it was! Was it my beloved Bip's? The proletariat for whom prose would suffice? Surely, Bip wasn't into porn. Or was it the arrogant Marcel's? He would certainly expect poetry.

And in what language?

Why did I always feel I was failing the audition?

Why couldn't we just be together, lie naked and let our energies be our guide?

Finally, I realized something. No matter whose it was, he didn't want speech. He didn't want prose or poetry or porn. He didn't want words at all!

So I talked to it in its own language: the language of touch. I held it, fingered it, rubbed it, stroked it. I coaxed it out of hiding in the language of silence. I kissed it, took it into my mouth, encircling its rosy head with my tongue, uttering melodious French cu-cu's of encouragement.

All the while the voice in my head was saying, "For God's sake, Marcel!" And, "God knows where you've been dipping this wick since Detroit." And, "You get my self-consciousness about my appearance, and I get a man who can't rise to the occasion." I felt the loneliness of the younger woman with an older man whose penis is refusing to perform.

A new day was upon us, a new day of another goodbye for another God-knew-how-long. Another closure too soon. Another packing away of if-onlys into the memory palace of illusion.

We parted company and I never got breakfast because I didn't want to be seen in public with Marcel looking as I did. It seemed like a loss in many ways, but beyond the fantasies and expectations of either of us was the bond that reconnected between us. It wasn't what either of us had fantasized, but it was real and it bought us another thirty-four years of endearment and adoration and interaction with one another.

Chapter 18
Joining the Crowd

Bluebeard stored his wives in a closet where they withered and died. Picasso kept his wives apart lest they kill each other. Marcel comped his women the best seats in the house, right next to each other, and expected us all to enjoy the show.

I found it awkward at first. The introductions inevitably led to the "How do you know Marcel?" Q & A's, which led to our respective positions and experiences with him. Women love to share stories with one another, and they *will* talk. Marcel didn't seem to care what we said about him, so long as we talked about him. Marcel took it all in stride and expected us to adapt. He treated us all like his extended family. There was no choice in the matter. He didn't have time to deal with the emotional dramas, and besides, tidiness was not one of his virtues.

Marcel may have had no back-up for his one-man show onstage, but there was always another woman, waiting in the wings, ready to step in should the current woman fall short. In his template where the theater was the real marriage, everyone was replaceable.

After the Medusa fiasco, I was downsized from being the catch of the day to the flavor of the week to the reminiscence of a valentine. At one of his performances in San Francisco, I found myself sitting side by side with a beautiful young woman from Texas, Anne, who turned out to be his current significant other. Rumor had it she was an oil heiress. We liked each other at once, but I couldn't help feeling the bitter aftertaste of replacement. Marcel was having a grand night on stage. There we were, Anne and myself, side by side, enjoying his show like the best of friends on a night out at the theater. There we were, Anne and me, part of the Marcel collection, as he performed his masterpiece, "The Public Garden."

It was set in a bygone era of elegance and stateliness, when people strode the walkways of a public garden to see and be seen on a Sunday afternoon. The men tipped their top hats to the ladies in passing. Children played with hoops and sticks and delighted in bouncy balls.

The skit opened with Marcel mounted on a low pedestal, a statue witnessing the parade of life. With a quick turn of heel, Marcel became the groundskeeper, tidying up the walkway with an imaginary broom that issued sound from the sweeping arc of his foot. After another shift of character, Marcel was a proud father wheeling his baby in a perambulator, bobbing his head to and fro while babbling silent baby-talk. A snap of attention and Marcel was a man pulled in all directions by his dog on a leash, pausing to nod at two ladies, while—to his mortification—the ladies' attention is drawn instead to the dog relieving himself. A half-turn and Marcel became a pious priest reading the Scripture as he strolled, pausing only to make the sign of the cross.

Next he gender-shifted into the characters of two old women sitting slumped on an imaginary park bench. One knit and gossiped with gusto; the other mindlessly nodded with eyes half-shut, bored out of her skull. The knitting needles provided punctuation, like a music director's baton. Her head wagged from side to side, her animated eyebrows conveying a myriad of expressions: scandal, intrigue, haughtiness, and blame, all the while the knitting needles clickety-clacked right along in rhythm, switching with the arch of a finger from row to row. She never dropped a stitch. Finally, she looked over her shoulder to one side, paused in her knitting, then slowly and deliberately pointed an accusing finger in the direction of her maligned subject. See? Her! Over there! It was uncanny to see how precisely Marcel could inhabit the quirks of the feminine.

Next, he transformed into a vendor holding a large bunch of helium balloons, which added buoyancy to the vendor's stride. A child holding his mother's hand approached and chose a special balloon. The vendor singled it out, tied it with a bow to the child's wrist, in exchange for coins that he dropped into his vest pocket. Then the balloon worked its way loose and floated high into the imaginary sky as the child looked on, wailing. The vendor continued on his way, half-walking and half floating with his massive canopy of bobbing balloons.

No public garden would be complete without the lovers. Marcel quickly changed roles to become both of them, lost in an embrace. With his back to the audience, he wrapped his arms around himself. One hand twirled the curls of his hair, while the other sensually traced the outline of his torso, from shoulder to hip, until it veered off course to the hip pocket, containing a wallet. Skillful misdirection of fingering the hair allowed the thieving hand to deftly pickpocket the wallet. A reprimanding slap returned the wallet to its pocket and the caress continued.

The Public Garden concluded as it began, with the groundskeeper sweeping clean the pathway of the flow of life. Marcel mounted the pedestal once again to become the motionless statue observing, unblinking, all that passed before him.

In much the same manner, Anne and I continued to encounter each other at Marcel's performances. Our rendezvous' came to feel like regular reunions. We met each other's sons, we kept track of who was doing what. I came to think of us both as a couple of moths that had flown into the fire of Marcel's sun, and rather than get burned alive, we befriended each other for support in a bond of sisterhood.

Years later, I received a letter from Anne, quite unexpectedly.

She wrote me from Paris at a time when Marcel nearly died on tour in Russia.

Dear Paulette,

Please forgive this letter is from me instead of Marcel, but I wanted you not to worry and to feel fine about him. He has received so many wonderful and loving messages that we are trying to answer them all. I am doing as many for the people I know personally as I can for him.

Joining the Crowd | 113

> *He is improving every day, but he is still a little weak. He lost much blood and 20 pounds. However, he is already putting it back on and looks better and better each day.*
>
> *Your card meant very much to him as he loves you so very much. I am sure it won't be too long before you can see him for yourself! It will amaze you to see how rested he looks.*
>
> *Do not worry. He has had a big shock and it frightened him, but he is fully capable of complete recovery—to work again. We have cried a lot together just because we are so happy he is safe.*

[She went on to describe Marcel's four weeks of recuperation—no phones, no visitors, and proper diet—and how badly he was frightened by his hospitalization.]

> *Please continue to send your prayers, love, and energy. It will help more than you know. All of his family appreciates your good thoughts, but especially Marcel and me.*
>
> *I also hope to see you soon again.*
>
> *My best regards to you and your son too!*
>
> *Love,*
> *Anne*

Marcel had been hospitalized with a perforated ulcer from stress while on tour in Moscow. In this experience, he overcame his lifelong fear of death by focusing instead on his mission in life: to spread the message of mime and seed it all over the world.

I was never summoned. I never saw Anne again. Marcel wrote to me, but we never spoke about it. These big life-altering experiences sank by weight of their own gravitas into the special locked chambers of his silent realm.

Chapter 19
Live the Death

"Live the death!" Marcel told his students at L'Ecole Internationale de Mimodrame de Paris, the mime school he opened in 1978. Death was a constant theme in Marcel's life. At the death camp of Auschwitz, it had stolen his father from him at an impressionable age. It had caused him to leave his mother behind in Limoges and move with his brother Alain to Paris, where they changed the family name from Mangel to Marceau, after François-Séverin Marceau, a French general who distinguished himself for bravery during the French Revolutionary wars.

Writer/poet Dana Negev gives a poignant description of the war years in Paris: "For four years they spent living in fear, using words as codes, each night sleeping somewhere else, not knowing who to trust. One Resistance member did not know the identity of the other. All around were masked faces, masked names."

The specter of death led him to become a hero himself by altering the papers of young Jewish children and posing as a scout master to lead them out of France and into the safety of Switzerland.

The theme of death was so much a part of Marcel that he took control of its icy fingers and turned them into his art form. He chilled the hearts of his audiences with his many faces of death. He spoofed it in his imagery of the macabre. Marcel definitely had a dark side. Bip managed to escape death, but for Marcel, it was a constant reminder of the fragility of life.

Living the death became an exercise he practiced every night in many different skits: "The Cage," "Bip Remembers," "The Butterfly Catcher," "The Trial."

In his skit, "The Cage," a man suddenly finds himself trapped within the walls of a cage. With fingers flayed open like fans of exclamation marks, hand over hand he traces the shape and perimeters of the cage, from side to side to ceiling. He grabs onto bars that don't budge in his grasp. As desperation to escape overcomes him, the cage closes in on him, becoming ever smaller, ever tighter, ever more encompassing. The man becomes frantic for a freedom he can see and sense but not attain. As the piece ends, one hand passes through the walled barrier, just as the man collapses with his free arm dangling limp from the effort. Lights out! We are left to wonder if he survives his desperate struggle or if he dies in the process.

"The Trial" is the plight of the defenseless on the game board of power, ego, arrogance, and apathy. In this tragic piece, Marcel takes us inside a courtroom. The bored-to-death judge can barely stay awake in his position of power over the life of a scared-to-death indigent defendant. The judge swivels his head from side to side, as if following the ball in a ping-pong match, as the lawyers argue, not over the fate of the defendant, but about who'll win the game. Then Marcel expresses the pathos and angst of the defendant, his life on the chopping block and his family and children at stake. We feel the crowning shock of his helpless disbelief as a guilty verdict is proclaimed. A swift edge of a hand gesture passes across the throat as if to indicate the blade of death. The man's head drops to his chest from the weight of utter hopelessness. The pitiful man is dragged off in chains to his death. Black out!

As bullets and bombs once bombarded the streets of war-torn France, so too does Bip relive the nightmare of World War II, every night on stage, in "Bip Remembers." Bip bravely runs with his rifle poised, in a desperate attempt to escape the flashing cross-fire from one side of the stage to the other. At one point he appears to be shot, but with Marcel's deftness of illusion, it quickly becomes apparent that his buddy actually took the bullet. With his back to the audience and his arms crossed in front of him so that only the hands appear from the rear, we perceive that he is holding the body of his dying buddy in his arms. We see the arm and hand of the wounded soldier grasping the air one last time before falling limp in the spasm of death.

Whereas most people would distance themselves as much as possible from such life-shattering memories, Marcel etched them ever deeper into his own consciousness, as well as the minds of his audience. Marcel insisted his audience remember the horrors of war and of death.

"The Butterfly Catcher" begins in a lighter vein, with the playful chase and capture of a fluttering butterfly in a net. The audience identifies with this common theme of childhood delight. But then Marcel puts a twist on it. Manhandled by the hapless catcher, the delicate wings of the beautiful butterfly flutter in the desperation of their last sign of life before the stillness of death overtakes it.

Marcel "managed" death by becoming its puppeteer. Its presence was always with him, but he held the strings.

Chapter 20
The Price to Pay

Although he was always surrounded by people, to me, Marcel's life seemed solitary. He was a prisoner of his fame. He was restricted in the freedom of movement that most of us take for granted. I always wondered if he ever equated his skit "The Cage" to his own life? And where does the feeling of "aloneness" come from? To me, it seemed to be because his vortex of self was so all-consuming that there was no room for anyone else. Marcel was not one to share the spotlight, onstage or off.

As a relevant aside, his powerful skit, "The Cage," was conceived by one of Marcel's most creative students, Alejandro Jodorowsky, who later went on to become an acclaimed underground filmmaker and actor/director. He's best known for *El Topo* (1970), which he directed and starred in, and *The Holy Mountain* (1973). Although I learned of Jodorosky's inception of this brilliant piece from Marcel, he never credited Jodorowsky in any way. When I asked Marcel why he didn't credit Jodorowsky for the concept of one of his strongest pieces, his response was, "Anybody can conceive of an idea. It is the one who puts it into action to whom the credit is due." Perhaps in payback, Jodorowsky credits Etienne Decroux as being his teacher of mime, while giving no mention to Marceau (in Jodorowski's listing on Wikipedia.)

Perhaps it was this quality of always claiming credit for himself, rather than sharing the credit that was due to others, that made Marcel seem like such a loner to me.

Also from my perspective, Marcel's life, indeed, seemed like a cage from which he could not (or would not) escape. Even if he did want, from time to time, to emerge from the cage, its walls closed him in, reminding him of the perimeter of his limitations. So, too, his whiteface—known to all the world—became the mask that expressed every human emotion onstage but almost always disguised the way he actually felt.

Conversely, everything he experienced turned into grist for his show. "The Mask" and "The Cage" were just as much self-portraits as "The Fallen Angel." Ironic? Not really. To Marcel, problems were never something to be fixed but material to be used.

Although Marcel tried to root his life with marriages and family, nothing much stuck. Nothing took precedence over or competed with his first and true marriage: the theater. Yes, he married once, twice, and a third time and had four children, but I always saw him as a remote center of the cyclone of handlers, entourage, and hangers-on that surrounded him. Did he not share his life in the conventional sense because he didn't want to or because it was not his to share?

In this day and age of celebrity worship and obsession over the lives and times of media superstars, too many people believe that it's enviable to be with someone famous. The money, the fame, the fans, the bling, and the glamour of being in the spotlight all have an appeal, but to me it's fool's gold—the false value of glittering surfaces, with a price that's too high for a payoff that's too fleeting. Being loved and adored by fans (basically strangers) provides a particular sense of fulfillment, but at the end of the day, one can't go home to an empty theater.

In that sense, my values differed vastly from Marcel's. To me, creativity is its own reward. On the other hand, the genius of Marcel cannot be judged by terms of normalcy. He lived on his own terms. He was always true to himself. My father used to say, "Genius is the height of selfishness with purpose." Marcel's purpose was mime: to seed, water, and nurture the message of mime throughout the world.

Many people close to him fell along the wayside of the journey, myself included. If he seemed caged, if he died without a partner by his side, that was the result of the choices he made, the sacrifices for and payoffs of superstardom, the constant chasing after, running from, and basking in the iconic image of Marcel Marceau, the world's greatest mime.

Chapter 21
Stillness, Essence, and Restraint

Marcel used to say, "To be a mime, one must be a sculptor, painter, writer, poet, and musician. One must also have incredible physical stamina. It's not dance. It's not slapstick. It is essence and restraint."

When I first met Marcel, the essence of the restraint inherent in mime was embodied by his "co-star," Pierre Verry. Pierre encountered Marcel when they were both students of Etienne Decroux in 1947.

They became friends and Pierre signed up with Compagnie de Mime Marcel Marceau in 1951 when it was performing at the Studio des Champs Elysée. He remained a faithful member of Marcel's entourage for twenty-six years, accompanying Marcel on nearly every world tour, where he remained until 1979 as Marcel's Presenter of Cards. It was a small but important role, and the only onstage role involving another person other than Marcel. Pierre's presence set the stage by introducing each skit imprinted in the form of a large placard, manually held with outstretched arms for an impossible length of time. Pierre's presence provided the vital stillness from which Marcel's dynamic exploded.

Pierre appeared in major roles of each of Marcel's mimodramas produced annually, the best known of which was "The Overcoat" by Gogol. His miming in the role of a Baron in "The Pawn Shop" led to the comparison with Daumier. He later headed Marceau's International School of Mime.

In T. Daniel and Laurie Willet's homage to Pierre, they write, "Pierre was one of the few people who had worked with both Marceau and Decroux, giving him a perspective unlike anyone else." Marcel, it is said, was Decroux's star pupil. When Marceau opened his mime school in Paris, Pierre became the director.

In the course of their twenty-six years of working together, Pierre toured the world with Marcel for twenty-five of them. To my knowledge, he is the only performer whom Marcel considered of equal caliber to himself and with whom he was frequently photographed, including in the photo with President Jimmy Carter.

Pierre was a dear, shy man, quite the opposite of Marcel's extrovert personality. But once you reached out to touch him, you found an endearing and enduring delicacy. He was a star of a different sort, whose radiance could be seen in the twinkle in his eyes. That radiance within his stillness was the first to light up the darkened stage. The combination of Pierre Verry and Marcel Marceau was untouchable.

Pierre's greatness did not have the same meteoric qualities as Marcel, but he projected plenty of power and vitality on stage. His was the discipline of patience, of stillness. He could hold impossibly difficult poses for an excruciating length of time, with never a quiver. Non-movement is as important as any other quality in the art of mime.

Stefan Niedzialkowski remarks about non-movement in his book *Beyond the Word: The World of Mime*, "Often we are impressed by the wonderful movements of a performer, but we also often fail to realize the importance and the profound strength of no-movement. These frozen pictures are part of the artistry of the mime. In every action of the performer, there are different kinds of stops. Before movement occurs, there is the stillness which is linked to concentration, and there is also the immobility out of which the beginning of movement is created. These stops within the performance are not only essential for the actor; they are essential for the spectator to be able to follow what the actor is trying to do.

"No-movement is like a still-life picture. The eyes cannot blink; breath cannot be visible; fingers and toes must be frozen. In fact, there is not even the slightest twitch of the body or the face. The actor becomes still. This is not, however, a picture of death. Even in absolute stillness, the energy of the living human being will betray life. To the mime, the stop is not a pose or an empty gesture; it is an authentic state of being for that moment. It is a moment that holds valuable energy, but for that moment the energy does not flow.

"No-movement, as a picture of the inner state of being, is the coordination of the physical state of existence with the psychological state of existence. It is absolute inner concentration existing in harmony with the outside world. Inner peace is visible through no-movement with the body positioned in a state of readiness. Stillness becomes silence, peaceful and crisp, like the surface of an undisturbed pond. During this concentrated state, the mime cleanses himself. From the center, energy emanates equally throughout the body. During the moment of no-movement, the mime experiences a unique physical and psychological self. It is like the moment of silence before an orchestra begins to play. At that moment, the audience, the orchestra, and the conductor experience the same state of readiness and concentration. Out of that state of readiness, the mime is able to begin his silent concert."

For though there is no art without inspiration, there is just as surely no form without technique.
—Marcel Marceau

In 1982, I was living for a time in Woodstock, New York, studying mime, when Marcel appeared in Manhattan. I attended the show and immediately noted that Pierre had been replaced by a much younger mime.

Though the part Pierre played in the show was small, I felt that the darkness of the stage without his radiant presence was big, and I was shocked to suddenly find him replaced by a younger man. What on earth happened? I wondered if Marcel had thrown one of his tirades and replaced all that was sacred, making room for the new, or if Pierre had left the stage to return to teaching in Marcel's School of Mime in Paris.

My initial suspicion was that some trauma or falling-out had occurred. The world isn't kind or generous to aging mimes. Mime is a singular mountain and Marcel was at its absolute pinnacle. Anything else would be a downhill slide on a slippery slope. I wondered if Pierre had faded like the gentle star of concentrated energy that he was into the dark and all-encompassing void of a broken-hearted silence to his unblinking devotion. As it turned out, he'd simply retired with his wife to the countryside outside of Paris. I was relieved that it was an amicable and not a quarrelsome or heartbreaking parting.

I wrote him this letter:

26 March, 1982
My Dear Pierre,

I have just been with Marcel in New York. His greatness is shining bright as ever, but the impact of the spectacle in general has lost much of its magic without you. You may have often felt that the part you played was small, but the darkness of the stage without the radiance of your presence is BIG. Someone else may be taking your place, but your presence has not been replaced. Your vitality, your heart, your soul, and especially your subtle humor is now an immortal memory. You brought a largeness to your role that is no longer there. Helas, Life continues to flow like the river that it is, and people come and go, but I can only say I am infinitely grateful to have experienced le spectacle de Marceau when the first moment of the opening curtain was Pierre Verry! It was a revelation of the power of mime in all its glory!

I hope that your life in the countryside is beautiful and fulfilling, as I'm sure you always dreamed it to be in all those long years on tour with Marcel.

My love for mime is finally being realized in lessons. Now that my role as a mother is no longer demanding my time I can turn totally to my art and to mime. At the moment, I'm living in Woodstock, NY, where I am studying mime with Maggie Green. We speak of you always, embracing you with each thought.

You are very loved and very missed, Pierre. I hope that somehow, somewhere our paths will cross again so that our eyes can speak again in the silence of understanding. I wish for you and your wife all the best.

Affectionately always,

Paulette

CHAPTER 22

Healing

It was twelve years down the road now, April 1984. Marcel was sixty-two. I was forty-seven. Marcel was in San Francisco for a four-week run at the Curran Theatre. My excitement started mounting long before he arrived. I was in a tizzy for weeks ahead; his meteoroid was orbiting in my constellation once again.

    I drove to San Francisco on the Monday preceding Tuesday's opening night, to visit with my dear friend Tony Cassanova, Marcel's stage manager. We had a five p.m. rendezvous. I went backstage where the crew was setting up; I was told that Tony had just left and to check his hotel up the block. He wasn't there either. I returned to the theater, then back to the hotel—no Tony. This was in the days before cell phones, so every dead end was a zig and a zag on foot. Also, it was unlike him to disappear like that. Our friendship was something precious to us both. It began back in the Detroit days and grew ever stronger over time. Tony considered me as "family."

    Finally Jerome, Marcel's young mime assistant, suggested I check the bar across from the theater. Of course! I should have thought of it myself; Tony was a drinker.

    Sure enough, there he was, lost in a haze of smoke, well soused, awaiting me with open arms. Though he spun around on his bar stool to give me a bear hug, I could immediately see that things weren't good with him. He had dark circles around his eyes, his olive skin was pallid, and his spirit was hardened. We sat for what seemed like a smoke-filled eternity while Tony downed one scotch and soda after another as I probed to get to the heart of the matter. His nerves were frazzled, burnt out. He was being consumed by the scavengers of negativity; his mood intensified from bad to worse with alcohol and cigarettes, until it leveled out in an arena utterly vile and morose.

After twenty-five years of service with Marcel, Tony had nothing good to say about him. He was also angry; he had spent the better part of the day doing work for which he would not be paid. Tickets were not selling as well as expected, sales were down, money was tight, nothing was right. Everyone was on edge, most of all Marcel. Tony sought solace in drink. As stage manager, his only leverage for getting paid was to threaten to cancel the four-week San Francisco run.

"The tour hasn't been going well. The theaters are only half-full. The money isn't pouring in as it should. The ticket prices are too high. Marcel himself is so concerned about his money problems that his concentration on stage is off. It's a vicious circle."

He paused for a gulp of scotch and deep drag on yet another cigarette. The ashtray was already mounding over. "I'm disgusted with the whole scene, the life, Marceau's craziness. I hate the way he treats people who are close to him, who care about him, starting with me and ending with you! Marcel doesn't want real friends, only people who flatter him. I've had it!"

I felt like I was witnessing history before my eyes: the fall of the king, the great master, the father of modern mime in America, the avatar of mime in the world.

After he downed his umpteenth drink, I took his arm and unfastened him from the bar. We walked for miles of this up-and-down city in an attempt to get him to unwind, to climb out of this quicksand of negativity. By evening's end, I was both wired and exhausted; Marcel's disequilibrium had knocked me off kilter as well. I deposited Tony back at his hotel and gladly drove the hundred miles home in the still of night just to return to my little life in the country, to my little farm of organic sanity.

The next night, I was still too drained to return to San Francisco for Marcel's opening. I heard the turnout was poor. Marcel was depressed. Tony was beside himself. For him, the only thing worse than threatening to close the show for personal reasons was for it to close prematurely for lack of attendance.

I went to the performance two nights later. I entered the theater fully expecting the worst. I brought flowers for Marcel: a single yellow rose in remembrance of the long-stem yellow roses he gave me on our first night together, and a fragrant gardenia, a symbol of delicacy that's fragrant and beautiful.

Marcel received me briefly in his dressing room while making up. He was covered only in his black kimono. His face was all white, without the final punctuation of the black eyeliner and red lipstick. He looked like a death mask of himself. Normally, Marcel never allowed anyone to see him when he was putting on his makeup; that space was inviolable. It was his time of stillness, meditation, and transformation.

I looked at him in this special moment. Once again the aura of his charisma stood my hair on end. I loved that face. Always had. I never tired of looking at him. His expressions were ever changing, sometimes young, sometimes old, sometimes handsome, sometimes grotesque, sometimes reflecting fear or horror, arrogance or anger, not even limited by gender. They were never static or staid. But now he was in neutral, sitting there before the mirror rimmed in bright lights that revealed every detail, with vats and vials of makeup before him. His radiance was rendered even more luminous by his whiteface, as he channeled the energy necessary to illuminate an entire theater. His deft hands were steady as he applied the black accents to his eyes, eyebrows, and lips. His eyes narrowed as he ran through various facial expressions to confirm that everything was as it should be.

Reflected in the mirror was the metal clothes rack with his costumes, arrayed in multiples. A row of Bip's classic burlap top hat, with its drooping red rose, sat atop the rack. There were also many dance slippers in gray and in black. He exchanged his slippers for new ones for every performance, after they'd stretched out too much to be worn again.

There it all was at a glance, the magical chamber wherein the man transformed himself into the legend.

Marcel gave the performance his all. I'd brought two local mimes with me, Rainbow and Jonathan Keeton, as my guests, a threesome all

Healing | 129

clumped together in fourth-row-center seats that Marcel comped us; we were a collective nerve line of excitement.

The rest of the audience was comatose.

Marcel seemed to be playing just to me, or was it that it just always felt that way? When his intense gaze bore into me, it was as though an entire theater filled with people disappeared and there was nothing but the two of us, alone, with his energy coursing through me, working me over, through and through, igniting every chakra. I imagined it to be like having sex in a crowd where the focus and concentration is so intense that no one else exists.

As I sat there, sandwiched between my two favorite local mimes in the best seats in the house with Marcel Marceau playing just to me, I was overcome with a feeling of gratitude: this was clearly one of life's best moments! The performance was powerful, electrifying, poignant. I was totally done in at the end of it. We jumped to our feet with applause. We were the only ones that did. The rest of the audience remained stupefied. They didn't get it. They could hardly raise their hands to applaud. I sensed Marcel's great disappointment as he took his bow. It was more than humility; it was heartbreak.

This program of Marcel's had been a surefire success for decades. But now it was as though the audience was bored with it. They wanted something more, but what?

The following morning, I was so moved by the irony of it all that I wrote Marcel a letter on my napkin at breakfast. A letter of love, friendship, and strength-giving encouragement. He needed a real lift, not just flattery. Our friendship was on its twelfth year. Our connection was not only real, but vital.

12 April 1984
My beloved Marcel,

You were in such a tizzy last night it was difficult to thank you and to tell you how much I loved your performance!

The new pieces—especially Bip, Star of a Traveling Circus—is sheer delight! Enchantment itself. Bravo!

Even though you were playing to an audience in a coma, still, you are as electric as ever. Each time I feel I have discovered you all over again for the first time. I am inspired, exalted, touched to my depths, filled with mad joy, excitement, and folly. It was perhaps a mistake to lower yourself in the last piece to the audience's "understanding" and then judge the result by the applause. Better to measure it by the goose bumps on my skin. Does the sun shine less brightly for the blind?

You and your work are as exciting, as powerful, and as inspiring as ever. It is important not to out-price the young. However barbarian and decadent our world has become, still, the young are the only fresh breath we've got, and your message is one of eloquence, hope, humor, love, and endurance—one can never get enough of that. It should be available for everyone. And even though the pieces are, well, vintage, so is Mickey Mouse! Time doesn't dim quality.

I know you've had some disappointments lately, and I know it's hard not to take that personally, but it's been a difficult time for everyone—astrologically, it's a wonder things aren't worse!

You have been a guiding force and inspiration for me again and again, and I will be the same for you whenever you need it. Thank you for playing for me last night—I felt it deeply. I was profoundly moved, and I love you always,

Paulette

The next time I saw the performance, Marcel was less potent, but the audience was alive and engaged, so all in all, he was pleased. Like many artists of the theater, an appreciative audience meant more to

Marcel than a great performance. He lived for that caress of applause. It was his lifeline.

That night at the bar, Tony was on quite a different drunk: this time he couldn't praise Marcel enough.

"This is a wonderful man, a big man, a truly great man. *This* is a man of size and I love him! Twenty-five years we've been together! This man is so generous, you can't imagine: he doesn't spend two hundred dollars on his friends, or two thousand, but two hundred thousand! Money means nothing to him. He only cares about his art!"

Ah, the many faces of alcohol.

I brought Tony and Paco, Marcel's lighting manager, home to my farm on their day off. We had a wonderful day. We hiked and picniced in a meadow overlooking the vast view, smoked a little weed, and laughed till it hurt. With it came a loosening of all those knotted tensions.

All talk centered around Marcel, but this time it was with fondness and nostalgia, of the days when ticket lines started at nine in the morning and went around the block, when success was easy.

When we returned to San Francisco that evening, we passed the Curran Theatre with its striking poster of Marcel Marceau: A LEGEND IN HIS OWN TIME. The the bold marquis flashed "For FOUR Weeks Only."

Tony sighed wistfully as we drove past. "I wish there was a SOLD OUT sign across the ticket booth."

My last dinner with Tony during the four-week San Francisco run was one of closely linked friendship between us, plus deep love for and mutual devotion to Marcel. As we sat at our table in the Empress of China restaurant overlooking the city lights, we both vowed that no matter how badly he treated us, his gifts of intimacy, confidence, and artistic genius outweighed any impulsive action or moment of weakness from him that might mar or affect us in some way. Our lives were totally changed because he took us in. We would travel any distance to be there for him when he needed us. All our complaints were nothing compared to the loyalty and devotion we both felt.

Over the years, Tony and I had become confidantes. Tony told me that when Marcel and I had first met in Chicago, Marcel had confided in him, revealing our intimacy.

"He told me *all* about it!" Tony exclaimed.

"How was I?" I twinkled.

"Grrrrreat!" He sounded like Frosted Flake's Tony the Tiger.

I felt much better to know Marcel was as bursting with talk as I at that time, for I, likewise, had immediately written everything down in my journal, like a schoolgirl on a first date.

After Tony and Paco's rave reviews about their visit to the farm, Marcel agreed to come for a visit of his own.

It was his day off and this was to be our one day together. I so wanted it to be nice. I was excited to share with him my California, my alternative lifestyle on the farm, my son Nicholas, and for once, a glimpse of who I was.

I was to pick him up at his hotel at nine a.m. Nightmarish morning rush-hour traffic in San Jose and San Francisco caused me to be a half-hour late.

As I entered the revolving doors to the hotel, I caught sight of Marcel at the far end of the cavernous lobby of plush maroon velvets and antique tables that gave off the scent of English lemon oil. He was wearing a maroon shirt, unbuttoned to his sternum; his beige pants were revealingly tight at the crotch (*tres Francais*), and he was sporting soft Italian loafers designed for deep carpets. Perfect for Paris and the high rollers of San Francisco, but rather inappropriate for a day in the country at a farm on a mountain. His casual beige cardigan made his pale skin, which rarely saw the light of day, look like uncooked dough.

Marcel was pacing the floor in the lobby like a pent-up beast when I arrived. I interrupted him in mid-stride to greet him and offer my apologies for being late.

He exploded on contact without even looking at me or tossing me as much as a "Bon jour." He was in a full-on purple rage. It was a head-turner. People were whispering and staring.

I was stunned. I looked around to see if he might be targeting someone else, but no.

I immediately wished we could take it again from the top, where I walked into the lobby and greeted him, and this time turn it into a comedy. No chance of that.

Then I turned back the pages of my mind for a moment, to review the situation to see if I'd missed something crucial. "Gee, is it because I'm late that he's so irate? Was it really all that critical to be absolutely punctual?"

Of course, I quickly realized that this wasn't about me. I was just the catalyst that put him over the top. I was the lucky one who drove two hours to be at this right place at the wrong time.

His rage, this endless geyser from center Earth, erupting all over the hushed elegance of this old-world hotel lobby, had been triggered by some two-bit mime magazine. Apparently, *Mime Review* published a big article about mime in America, and Marcel's name was never even mentioned! Here he was, the world's avatar of modern mime, especially in the United States. No one had ever done so much for mime in the twentieth century as Marcel Marceau. It was a major oversight or faux-pas on the part of the magazine's editor. It was like writing about royalty in England and omitting mention of the Queen.

Marcel was inconsolable, and try as I might, I couldn't deflect or distract or mitigate the impact of his raw fury. On a previous occasion when he had hurt me, my wounded ego proclaimed "Never again," and I found solace by gloating over the fact that at least I wouldn't have to be the one to pick his illustrious white face off the floor when the time came that he bombed. No such luck! I was the *only* person who could put Humpty Dumpty together again, because I was the only one who wasn't afraid of him. Yes, I still believed he was a god, but unlike everyone else who treated him like one, in my own way, I considered myself his emotional equal. When you stand alone at the top, few people look you in the eye. I was one of them.

Without saying another word, I took him by the arm, packed him and his live tantrum into my car with the bale of hay in the back to absorb the shock waves, and away we went, wheeling the ups and downs of the streets of San Francisco in this pressure chamber on wheels in morning traffic. Marcel was strapped in beside me, the same man who filled entire theaters with the power of his silence, now an enraged maniac, the volume turned up to high decibels, sitting two feet away. It was hard to concentrate on the traffic with him yelling like that at such close range. He started to sound like he was having a break with reality. But what *was* reality when everything was illusion?

So there we were: Marcel Marceau yelling uncontrollably, while I was trying to see over the steering wheel and hood of my car up the steep tilt of the hills.

Once the car was on the coast road, with a roaring ocean on one side and high cliffs on the other, I rolled up the windows and fought his fire with my fire, dragon to dragon. As loud as I could, point blank in his face, I yelled, "Shut up!"

I called him every name in the book for being so stupid as to confuse himself with a two-bit article. Then I softened the blow. "To think that anything anyone could ever say would ever begin to describe what you are to mime! You're the body, the brain, the spirit, and soul of modern mime. Anyone who wishes to become a mime must first either copy you or be as innovative as you. No one has even come close! All contenders disappear in your shadow!"

I met intensity with intensity, but not as a negative force in opposition to him. Rather, I presented it as a supporting strength. It was the right thing to do; my words had the effect of a gunshot into the air. It was as though he'd been tazered. His eyes lost their fury and became glazed. He blinked at me in silence with the expression of a child surfacing from the grip of a nightmare. From one instant to the next, he became silent, then sighed, and said, "Among true friends, there's no need for conversation," whereupon he took my hand, kissed it, smiled lovingly, placed his head on my shoulder, and fell sound asleep for the remainder of the trip, his hurricane all played out.

He slept through two picturesque hours of the drive. He missed the magnificence of the central California coast, resplendent with a thousand suns and windsurfers spinning wheelies on the rooster tails of waves; the verdant green fields, acres of wildflowers, stately redwoods, and Cyprus trees bowing down from the wind; the forests and patchwork farms vibrant with green, edging the Prussian blue of the Pacific Ocean laced whitecaps. He slept through it all. The tamed beast was too tuckered out to notice a thing.

When we drove into Santa Cruz, Marcel awoke with a ravenous hunger.

I smiled to myself, thinking, this guy is like a child who only rages, sleeps, and eats. The only thing he hadn't done yet was pee. I pulled up to a little mom-and-pop health-food store on the edge of town to get him some fruit and yogurt. His digestive system was no longer the invincible garbage disposal it used to be.

I asked him if he wanted to wash the fruit.

"No!" he said. "I never wash fruit. The pesticides kill the parasites."

Indeed, he was rarely sick, in spite of his nonstop round-the-world travels.

We were standing in the short line to pay when a lightning bolt struck.

Some hippie surfer behind us exclaimed, "Oh my God! Aren't you Marcel Marceau?"

It was the voice of an all-knowing and benevolent God, reaching down in the form of an anonymous stranger in Nowhereville USA, to validate the existence of Marcel Marceau as a household name, even out of the theater, out of whiteface, out of any and all context whatsoever. The mime magazine didn't do it, but here in a health-food store on the edge of Santa Cruz, a relatively small California beach town known for its surfing and university, in that order, where we stopped by chance, he was seen and recognized for the world icon that he was! The twenty-something surfer wasn't even of his generation. It was an absolute *miracle*! In return, Marcel graciously autographed his grocery receipt.

The horrible demons that plagued Marcel's worst fantasies—that he was fading before his time and being obliterated off the charts of history as forgotten—retracted their hold on him and shriveled into nothingness. Ah! The power of illusion!

Once back in the car, Marcel fell asleep again. He slept through the last leg of the journey. He missed the beautiful apple orchards of this fertile part of California; the majesty of the redwood forests with the magical play of light and shadow on the giant ferns; the deer and birds; the rays of sunshine beaming through the trees like the hallelujah in a cathedral. His head bobbed from side to side like a tetherball as I drove the last two miles up Redwood Road outside the small town of Corralitos, along the bad dirt road with potholes, ruts, and hairpin turns, rounding the last spectacular curve that burst out of the shadowed forest into a vast expanse of openness with panoramic views of plentitude, with the orchard in our lap dipping into the valley below, all the way to the ocean. Grand vistas of mountains, lakes, orchards, and fertile valleys leading to the sea lay before us. Even the sky was grandiose, safe, and sheltering.

Good Day Farm was all green and flowery, twittering with spring life. Peacocks greeted us with their long train of iridescent blue tails fanned and shuddering; the horses came up to nuzzle; my son Nicholas was there to extend his greetings, as were dogs and cats and chickens everywhere. It was a grand welcome party.

Marcel stepped out of the car and nearly fainted. He was so weak—and probably overwhelmed—he could barely stand. Who knows what he saw or thought? His first words were, "Where is ze bathroom?"

The radiance of the moment switched to instant improv, and as I mumbled under my breath, "It's wherever you want it to be," Nicholas quickly overrode my remark with gracious aplomb, saying, "I'll take you there myself." He held him lightly by the elbow and with head held as high as English aristocracy, he escorted Marcel Marceau in his unborn-calf Italian loafers and tight pants and low-cut shirt through unkempt knee-high grass to the outhouse. The outhouse had a great view but no door, so Nicholas politely turned his back to give Marcel the privacy accorded one of his world-class status. When I later recounted this story to a friend he said, "Marcel Marceau in your outhouse! This I gotta see!"

I'd invited Marcel to come to my farm for twelve years. Now that he finally accepted, I no longer lived there, but the friends who were staying there pitched in to make the visit warm and welcoming. They occupied my handmade Cherry Tree House, which I built decades ago with a couple of creative, stoned-out hippies. The old-growth cherry tree, which grew through the floor and out the roof, produced cherries that fell into your bowl from its outstretched branches inside the cabin. One room was the kitchen, the other the bedroom. That was it. It had no indoor plumbing. The shower and claw-foot bathtub were outside under a redwood tree.

In keeping with Marcel's minimal eating habits, they prepared a simple meal of brown rice and home-grown steamed veggies, served with fresh home-baked bread, enjoyed al fresco in the orchard where I had originally composed my letter to him.

We picnicked on a weather-beaten redwood table beneath an endless expanse of blue sky that offset the green grass and yellow oxalis flowers that carpeted the orchard. We were joined by the horses and the peacocks and cats and gophers. Nothing threatened or aroused concern. Even nature was on its best behavior, warm and peaceful. It couldn't have been more embracing or inviting.

After lunch, Marcel needed another nap. He was exhausted to the core. He slept on my futon on the floor of the small bedroom with the potbelly stove in this handmade cabin. I wondered if, at some level, our relationship that began with my letter from the orchard had come full circle. Was this the healing that was needed: to return to the source and just let it go? If so, let the healing begin!

I had to commend him for being such a sport to reconfigure a lifetime of European high culture, world travel, and social ladder-climbing to the likes of Good Day Farm, where he used the outhouse and slept on a futon on the floor. Then again, sometimes what's needed is a nurturing change from cities and hotels and traffic and demanding schedules and frazzled nerves. Fame and fortune feed the ego but don't feed the spirit or nurture the soul. It takes a visit back to basics, back to nature, back to what's simple and true to fill the void. I wondered if he was visited in his dreams by the letters we exchanged back in the days before we met.

Seeing Marcel like that, a guest on my turf, reminded me of how awkward and out of place I felt with him on that brave and daring maiden voyage to Chicago. What goes around comes around. He validated me in his world, and I validated him in mine.

Marcel awoke all new and refreshed. The color had returned to his face. His eyes were filled with vitality and excitement. His equilibrium had been restored. He was grounded once again. When this intersection of three earth fault-lines wasn't wreaking havoc, the energy of Good Day Farm was especially restorative.

Nicholas and Marcel spoke of the Angel sculpture Marcel commissioned Nicholas to do of him. These two geniuses sparked each other's creative juices. He saw the cabin Nicholas built for himself at age sixteen. Every breath seemed to revitalize him deeper. He regained his stance, his connection to the earth.

It was a day of all give, no take. Everything was an offering.

Nicholas and Marcel discussing the sculpture at Good Day Farm

Finally, it was time to return Marcel to San Francisco. He was to be honored that night at a black-tie banquet at the French Embassy with the ambassador and dignitaries from the city.

We'd passed through a biggie on this day, which began with the loss of face, his illustrious whiteface known the world over being eclipsed by the power of illusion, the forceful shadow of his own insecurity. I met him at his own level, face to face, tirade for tirade, took him home to my world, healed his wounds, propped him back up, nurtured his depleted soul, and returned him in time for a black-tie dinner of a gala evening—to which he did not invite me.

It was one of those moments where I clearly saw my place in his life: I might have been his restorer, muse, lover, and friend, but I was not the woman on his arm at an important banquet.

Fantasy and reality have their social boundaries, after all, invisible though they may be to the naked eye.

Chapter 23
I Recall...

In the early days of our relationship, Marcel often invited me to come to Bercheres, his three-hundred-year-old farmhouse estate in the Loire region, about thirty miles outside of Paris. I always wanted to go, but could never muster the airfare, and Marcel never offered to send me a ticket. He never realized how tight money was in my life, and I never told him. It was never discussed. And because he was so sensitive about people always wanting something from him, I had no intention to ever fall into that category.

Still, he tossed out the invitation to visit him in France so often, I took it for granted that the invitation would always be there, but then many years passed without mention of Bercheres or "come visit." So the next time he did, I realized it was now or never. I desperately wanted to go, but equally important to me was that my son Nicholas get to know Marcel, this man whom I held in such high regard and who had so impacted my life.

Finally, good fortune smiled upon me, at least with a half-smile: I sold a piece of art to fund the trip, but for one airfare only. So I weighed the situation and sent Nicholas in my place. And Marcel, who had met my son the year before at my farm but didn't really know him, agreed to host seventeen-year-old Nicholas in my stead. Remarkable! Who would do such a thing? Once again Marcel showed his true colors of openhearted graciousness.

Nicholas spent three days at Marcel's home. They bonded like kindred creative spirits. At the end of that short time, Nicholas had imprinted on Marcel's ability to mime to the degree that Marcel invited him to join the show and be his presenter of cards. Other people would have killed for such an invitation, but Nicholas, whose passion was art, not mime or theater, graciously turned him down. He didn't want to live out his own promising life in such a huge shadow.

In 1985, I moved to New York for eight months to try to get work as a graphic artist with magazines. But the timing was all wrong. It was the beginning of a recession. The graphic artists I so admired were being laid off. My work received high praise from art directors, who dangled the carrot that they'd love to hire me when the economy improved, but compliments don't pay the rent or bills, especially in Manhattan. I needed work immediately, not if and when times got better.

To add to my misery, I discovered that my work was copied and appeared under the name of staff artists. New York is rich in crime, especially when times are tough. This form of thievery—stealing ideas and style—felt worse than getting mugged. I found it to be the deepest cut of all.

On days when I didn't have appointments with art directors, I put on my whiteface and costume to paint the faces of children at the carousel in Central Park, for pocket money. A man saw me in my get-up and engaged me in conversation. I told him I had to leave New York for lack of work.

He asked, "Would you stay in New York if you didn't have to pay rent?"

"What are you suggesting?" I asked.

"Well, you could stay with me," he said.

"Where would I sleep?" I asked, seeing where this conversation was headed.

"I only have one bed, but you could have whichever side you want!"

With that, I paid my rent on a credit card, tucked tail, and returned to my farm in California.

During this sojourn in New York, Marcel and I met again. He invited me to his show and to stay over with him afterward. I went along, knowing the routine: dinner at midnight, then back to his hotel, where he made hours of calls.

I was tired after a hard day of all that's hard about the Big Apple: the miles of walking on concrete, the hordes of people, the frowning faces, the closed doors of not getting hired for work, the grim determination of pitting oneself against people from all over the world who have come to New York with their own grim determination to make it by hook or by crook; the push-shove on subways and buses; the schlepping of three heavy portfolios of my work from here to there and back again. By day's end I was all done in.

I slipped into the one bed in Marcel's hotel room and caught up on my sleep while he made his calls. At about four in the morning he joined me.

"It's after four," I mumbled, glancing at my watch as he slipped into the perfect curvature of our bodies together.

"Among true friends, there is no time," he responded.

He held me close to him, and I took his hands in mine, feeling the natural blending of our bodies, not from the meltdown after high-powered sex, but from all that was right about us: the ease of just being together, the true humbleness of quiet moments like this, with nothing going on. I felt the power that we generated, the beauty, and the love. Our breathing and our heartbeats became one; we slept the sleep of a return to blessed innocence, with our bodies entwined and our heads touching.

Also in New York, I was stunned by the size and scale of his world fame, which was so apparent in that great city that loves greatness. (In 1999, New York declared March 18 Marcel Marceau Day.)

After a magnificent performance in the Bronx, he singled me out of the

sketch by Paulette Frankl

mob scene to exchange greetings, embraces, and whisper in my ear, "Call me at the hotel."

The next day, I drove with Tony and the stage crew to West Point, where Marcel was performing in the evening.

I was dozing when he came into the backstage lounge where I awaited him. The magnetism brought us together immediately. We began talking, first formally, then personally, with stories of our parents. It was so sweet, sitting there in that backstage lounge at West Point, exchanging backgrounds—an indication that we were finally getting to know something about each other. With Marcel, facts always followed perception. With us, it took a long time to get around to learning about the basic facts.

Then he took me by the hand and led me to the stage where the crew was doing lighting and sound checks for the evening performance. We walked onstage, arm in arm—his arm around my shoulder, my arm around his waist—back and forth, across the stage like a pendulum, talking about the years of our friendship, the intense beginning in '72, the deception of '73, the pride and ego of '74, the mending and reconsideration of '75, the cautious inchings back to zero of '76 through '79, risking to be lovers again in '80 and '81—and now the tenderness of '82.

The mood was rich, deep, wise, childlike, backed by the innocence

Inscription from book, The Story of Bip, *by Marcel Marceau*

of strength. We talked about jealousy, possession, and art, about the history of mime, politics, crooks, and criminals. Being with Marcel was an offstage program of boundless variety. His insatiable curiosity took in everything.

We found our adoration of each other again there, onstage, at West Point Military Academy (we both abhorred anything having to do with military), and we embraced like a classic moment in the cinema, like a theater performance, historical even, before an empty house with no audience.

This time together meant the world to me. After all, there we were, in his space, his altar, his temple, his marriage, his safe place: the theater—and I had the feeling he was now including me in his life of that special place in that special way. As I aspired to integrate the art of mime into my depths, this was my initiation into that world by the great master.

After the performance later that evening, Marcel was noticeably tired. His energy level didn't quite hit the mark; he was good, but not great.

However, riding back in the chauffeured car was enchanting. Ninety minutes of intense talk, with deep insights about towering figures: Picasso, Chaplin, Socrates, de Gaulle, even Alexander the Great.

Once back at the hotel, Marcel remained delightful. With the fervor of a child at Christmas, he rummaged through packages of food sent by fans, pulling out food for our private dinner in his room. Here in the grand elegance of his suite at the Regency, he laid the table for our feast. It felt like a celebration. He produced a bath towel and placed it on the elegant table, never unfolding it. On top of it, he piled little aluminum surprise packages of sweets and fruits sent by fans and admirers. On the top of the arrangement, he placed a huge bundle of grapes, still in their plastic bag! Marcel beamed with the proud radiance of a child at a party. He had *provided*!

Finally, the love-making. Marcel didn't make love *with* a person, he made love *to* a person. Always the loner, always the observer, always the controller, always maintaining a margin of separateness, even in sex. It was curious, but enjoyable. We pleased each other with great tenderness.

I often wondered what he saw in me that continued to bring us together again through time. Certainly, he recognized and respected the artist in me. But perhaps most of all, it was the honesty we shared, and the comfort of each other's presence. I always felt that Marcel was content in my company, which must have been a rarity in his position of fame and all its impositions.

A few days later, I sent Marcel a card for his sixty-first birthday.

Dearest Marcel,

When the candles of Time burn down to stars,
  And all the great moments of Life
    are but the blinking of lights,
      Your eyes will be
        Everywhere.

The years slipped by.

I read that Marcel would be appearing in an HBO concert with Michael Jackson, who developed his famed "moonwalk" after seeing Marcel's "walk against the wind" routine. The concert was cancelled after Jackson was hospitalized for exhaustion during rehearsals.

I met his sons. (Marcel had two sons by his first marriage, to Huguette Mallet. He and his second wife, Ella Jaroszewicz, had no children. But he had two daughters by his third wife, Anne Sicco.) He met my grandchildren when I brought them to his shows. As always, our lives took us in different directions: his of trying to mix marriages and family life with the all-consuming theater; mine of trying to land employment as an artist and/or performer. But the one constant was the magnetic pull of our bond. It always brought us together again, wherever that might be.

While Marcel was experiencing the upheaval of marriages, divorces, children, and alimony, I experienced the upheaval of the 7.1 California earthquake in 1989 that buckled and collapsed the upper level of the Bay Bridge in Oakland and destroyed large portions of the city of Santa Cruz and its environs. Its epicenter was just a short quarter-mile from Good Day Farm. It pretty much destroyed the farm. It broke all water lines, destroyed electricity, and totally demolished any trace of my five-thousand-gallon redwood water tank.

Water wars ensued. Lifelong friends who had formed alliances in a living community became arch enemies. We were all ready to turn one another in for illegal structures over the issue of water rights. It got very, *very* ugly.

I realized I could spend the rest of my life in therapy with these people, who had been the cornerstones of my life, or move on. I chose the latter. I relocated the animals, then moved north to the small town of Bolinas in west Marin County, north of San Francisco. There, I began a career as a courtroom artist and writer.

I lived that life for nine years, until the frustrations of trying to earn a living from my art and writing prompted me to take heed of the wise words of my magic mentor, Jeff McBride: "If you ever want to get anywhere in life, you have to get out of your comfort zone."

I took a look around and determined that my comfort zone consisted of beautiful people in beautiful places and a healthy lifestyle, no matter how uncomfortable the living situation. So I packed up my past and moved to Las Vegas, to join the merrymakers of magic in the magic capital of the world. I became one of the few working female magicians in Sin City.

Las Vegas was another planet. It was so foreign to my comfort zone that it made me question my sanity. I gave up friends, family, and everything beautiful and dear to my heart in exchange for making coins, cards, and balls vanish in my hand!

Ironically, the most magical thing of all was that Marcel and I met again in this sci-fi city of artifice inhabited largely by overweight aliens.

Marcel was invited to be the inaugural show for the grand opening of the Paris Hotel and Casino in Las Vegas in September 1999. The name Marcel Marceau was the symbol of everything French.

As always, my routine, life, and peace of mind all went into a tailspin in anticipation of seeing Marcel again. We hadn't been in communication for a very long while, long enough to stop counting. He wasn't aware that I'd taken up residence in Las Vegas.

I left word backstage that I'd be present at his opening performance and hoped he would make time afterward for a moment together. I also sent ahead a dozen roses.

The Las Vegas Paris was a dazzling array of lights. The replica half-size Eifel Tower never looked glitzier. Because of its brand-spanking newness, the interior of the casino smelled fresh, with no trace of the stale, sour air of cigarette smoke, booze, and money so common to Vegas casinos. The theater was its crowning glory, all that money could buy.

But if ever there was a culture clash, a total round peg in a square hole, it was Marcel Marceau playing Vegas.

He had performed to audiences the world over, under all sorts of difficult conditions, but this had to be the worst on earth bunch of theater-goers EVER! No amount of money spent on perfect performing conditions could make up for the world's crassest audience: totally uncultured, crude and rude, loudmouthed, boorish, and drunk to boot.

I felt as though I was witnessing the end of an era, an era that had elegance, class, meaning, beauty, and above all, subtlety. An era of substance. I felt as though a new breed of orks was trampling all that was precious and good.

These people had no finesse, no sensitivity, no ability to observe or concentrate or understand. If it didn't involve tits or ass or tigers or things that went boom, they weren't interested. This audience totally lacked heart and soul; they wanted only to be shocked, stunned, and blasted with artifice, the louder the better.

At its peak, mime was in sync with the tempo of the time. Over the decades, however, that changed. Technology brought with it speed and impatience. Audiences wanted ear-splitting sound, loud, explosive, deafening thrills. Rock 'n' roll amped to the max, heard from the first row, breaking the eardrums. No one had time nor interest for the finesse of mime. Life had geared up to the fast lane, and speed was what thrilled. Mime was a speed bump.

This Las Vegas audience personified all of that. It was boorish drunkenness at its worst. People openly spoke during the performance, or just staggered out from restless boredom before intermission, sloshing their oversized cocktails along with them. The level of insult was beyond measure. It was agony. It was a disaster. My heart broke to see Marcel in front of that crowd.

After the show, Marcel was so incensed he could hardly talk. He neither wanted to see nor be seen like that. Backstage, he gave me the perfunctory kiss-kiss on the cheek, thanked me for the flowers, and ran from the pain.

Even so, this 1999 tour, after fifteen years of shows that didn't sell out, marked a renaissance of Marcel's career, with strong appeal to a third-generation audience. It paved the way for him to bring his full mime company to New York City for the presentation of his mimodrama, The Bowler Hat, in 2000.

The following month, in October 1999, we were on the threshold of the new the millennium. My interaction with Marcel was now twenty-seven years old, and Marcel was seventy-six. He was once again playing San Francisco. I'd traveled up from Vegas to catch his show and (hopefully) have some time with him. I invited a longtime buddy, Marc, to the performance, who kindly let me stay at his flat in the city. I didn't ask Marcel to comp us seats. I paid like everyone else. After the show, Marc and I went to the Farralon Bar next to the theater for a nightcap. We'd just ordered drinks when Marcel appeared with friends and sat at a neighboring table.

Oh, the delicious fate of it! It reminded me of all the times I'd sat in the audience with his paramours, fighting the urge to retaliate. Ultimately, I did fight fire with fire, as I began to invite male friends to join me at his performances. When I introduced them to Marcel, I could sense the chill go up his spine. It gave me a twinge of satisfaction.

Again, on this evening, Marcel refused to be outshone or upstaged by the presence of my handsome young companion who was half his age. He appeared at our table and turned on the charm, eclipsing everyone in the room. Suddenly, it was as if no one else existed but Marcel and myself. He took my hand, kissed it again and again working his way up my arm. I took his hand, kissed every finger individually and passed it along my cheek. We were locked in a playful flirtatious exchange of smiles and delight to end all.

I was drinking a Brandy Alexander. Marcel wanted to taste it, whereupon he ordered *two* for himself! This was from a man who didn't even drink wine, let alone hard liquor. But I guess he assessed that this was a two-drink situation and threw caution to the wind. Without hesitation he slugged down the two Alexanders as though they were mini chocolate milkshakes in martini glasses. Then, emboldened by the alcohol, he went into a dance of seduction that would have been the envy of any peacock. He offered me his hand and led me to the center of the small room. By then, I had done enough mime to respond in kind, and had no inhibitions about playing along with him. We were moving in the small space between the tables, miming courtship together for the first and only time ever. Our thoughts were made visible by our actions and body language. We were like two kids, disobeying all the rules of social conduct right there in a public bar. Marcel filled the room with his charisma, completely obliterating the presence of my companion, who—unbeknownst to Marcel—had no interest in me as a woman. Marcel once said to me, "The older you become, the better you have to be." He was at his best. The room broke into applause.

"Meet me at my hotel tomorrow at four!" he called over his shoulder as he turned heel to make his exit.

I was beyond excited!

Marc worked as an event designer in the city, so he had license to purchase at the wholesale flower market. We went at six the next morning to load up with an extravagance of flowers for Marcel: roses, orchids, and bundles of tuberose. I wanted to make up for all the times when he was on the wing and I didn't have the means to shower him in the fragrant blooms of my adoration.

In my magic work in Las Vegas, I was mixing in mime, so I hoped Marcel would critique my moves to give me an edge in Vegas's competitive field of entertainment, and even write me a letter of recommendation for the jobs I sought. I was one of the only female magicians in Vegas, in fact, one of a handful in the world, but even at that, magic was a man's world and gigs were hard to get.

In anticipation of our rendezvous, I spiffed up my personal appearance to a professional gloss. I wore my most elegant décolleté black outfit that did good things to my toned performer's body; I even went all out and had my hair coiffed for the occasion. To top it off, I wore the beautiful Indonesian pearl pendant Marcel had given me on another occasion. For once, I felt presentable.

I arrived at the stunning Hotel Nikko ten minutes early with armloads of flowers, my video camera, and a bag of farm apples.

Marcel received me in the salon of his suite without even a gesture of greeting. He mumbled something in French that I couldn't understand. By this time, his hearing was already starting to go bad, so he was probably unaware of his own voice and how inaudible his mumble was to others. Continuing his mutter, he shuffled off into what I presumed was the bedroom. I thought maybe he had forgotten something, or that I had caught him napping, unaware that it was time for our appointment, although he appeared to be ready when I came. I couldn't imagine what was taking him so long. It seemed he was gone for ages.

When at last he returned, I noticed that his fly was unzipped and his clothes were askew. Was the mumble-jumble and the sideways nod of his head an invitation for me to join him for sex in the bedroom? Good God! We hadn't even said hello! Maybe I was stuck on this "hello" thing, but it seemed important to start *somewhere*. His abbreviated gestures spoke volumes onstage, but they didn't always translate in real life. It didn't occur to me at the time that mime was the language of essence, so what did I expect? Now he seemed disgruntled.

As a misdirection to my facial expression of surprise, he immediately said, "Show me your work."

Though taken aback, especially after our flirtations of the night before, I unloaded my cargo of flowers, camcorder, and apples onto his coffee table and proceeded to run through the opening effect of my magic routine, miming the props that I would normally use. My audition before the great master was neither my best nor the worst of my abilities, but given the circumstances, I felt okay about it.

"Sit down," he said after I was finished.

I expected him to dissect it gesture for gesture.

Instead, he began, "When I first started out, there was nothing but Bip against a black curtain, Bip walking against the wind, Bip climbing stairs. No one was doing that."

For forty minutes, he went on and on about himself!

A magnificent book had just been published about him, *Le Mime Marcel Marceau*, by Valerie Bochenek. He went through every page of this tome, turning one page at a time, pointing out photos of all the great people in the history of the world for whom he had performed. President Jimmy Carter was among them. Then he proudly showed me his drawing book, *Bip and the Butterfly*, about which we had brainstormed at an earlier time. He showed me the reproductions of his art, in which I noticed he had included an image of himself somewhere in every painting.

Part of me couldn't help wondering, what does any of this have to do with me? But once again, on a bigger scale, I realized this was a very special moment in the mosaic of life, which far surpassed my own little magic moves and clamoring ego.

After he'd exhausted his story and the book, we arranged the flowers together; it was a quaint little moment of domesticity.

"Place them into the vase one at a time," he ordered. "The Japanese do it one at a time"—always the director of every moment.

Finally, his attention turned to me and for the first time since I arrived, I felt the warmth of his gaze pour over me like warm honey. It was that same gaze that newborns need to receive to instill in them the assurance of a bonding love.

"Oh, you're good at this," he remarked, never breaking his gaze while pouring the vase of water all over the table. He made no effort to wipe it up until I told him to do so; I also noticed his agility in cleaning each flower, leaf, and stem, and clipping the stems, but leaving the clippings strewn all over the floor. I'd been raised by a Japanese, and I knew well the art of careful attention to detail. But none of this mattered, for we were once again lost in that magical spell of our togetherness, floating above time and space, speaking words, and making gestures with our hands and the flowers that were mere vehicles of the connection that was being formed, the weaving of our separate energies into togetherness, understanding, being, beyond words, into a shimmer of pure light.

And then it was time for me to go. Our allotted hour together was up. The show must go on. As the moment shattered and returned us to reality, I managed to remind him of my request for a letter of recommendation. He promised he would send it.

In parting he gave me the golden glow of his smile, and I gave

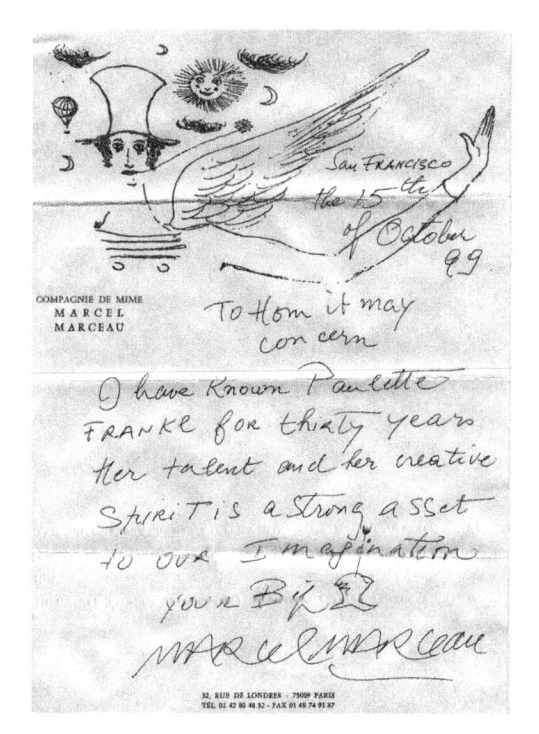

letter of recomendation from Marcel

him the golden radiance of mine. We each glowed in the goldenness of the gift of each other.

10/29/99
My dear Marcel,

I had abandoned hope until your letter arrived. I can't describe to you the joy I felt upon receiving it and your letter of recommendation. All the clouds of my life lifted and bright hope poured in. The invisible doors that can only be opened with song suddenly unlocked. I thank you from the depths of my heart.

It was so special to have an hour together with you in San Francisco, to walk through the pages of your beautiful book, to review your life, to experience your awesome career, one page at a time, and then to fill the room with flowers with you, one flower at a time. These are moments in the sea of a lifetime that I cherish forever and never forget.

Ah! Show biz! What an amazing chamber in the house of the imagination and of art. Your words of wisdom about each gesture bespeaking the entirety of one's soul was a precious gift to me. I hope that somewhere there is a book of your eloquent wisdoms and the poetry of your articulate expression, which is equally as impressive as your all-descriptive silence. You have mastered so many realms of communication. My soul is still resonant with the afterglow of our rencontre. This is the true "reality" in life, when all else fades.

The golden thread of our connection together, which began in 1972 and now spans three decades, has grown stronger in time. I hope that someday you will experience my magic onstage and feel touched by it, as I have been touched by you.

I always thought that someday, after the final curtain call, the last bravo, the last standing ovation, we would find each other again, and fill that cup that had been waiting so long and so patiently to be sipped in its entirety. But it was not meant to be. To hope for if-only's is to miss what is.

I am complete with the time that we shared.

Sometimes less is more.

I had asked him to share with me a moment of time, so that we might experience the infinite. He did that in spades. We forged a bond that was real and that spanned time. We will always be a part of each other, even if only in spirit. Nothing and no one can take that away.

Chapter 24
80th Birthday

When we met for the last time, it was for his eightieth birthday performance in Los Angeles.

It seemed that all of Hollywood turned out to pay him tribute. The line at the theater appeared to have no end.

His performance included "The Creation of the World," which was partly figurative, partly abstract. Marcel mimed the uncoiling of a plant tendril reaching upward toward the light, and the inception of fish, wherein he moved his hands in a curling undulation, with his thumbs protruding on either side, like fins. It was an astounding portrayal of a fish swimming. He mimed the flight of a bird, the way in which the head dips and pulls forward while the wings row the air. Lastly, he mimed the birth of man, Adam, and the snake offering the apple from the Tree of Knowledge.

He performed his skit "Youth, Maturity, Old Age, and Death," each stage in life distilled down to its particular posture, energy, and body language. At the end of this skit in the bent posture of old age, with its accompanying hesitant movements, Marcel shrank right in front of the eyes of his audience, becoming smaller and smaller as he walked into an imaginary vanishing point onstage. *Time Magazine* remarked of this piece, "He accomplishes in less than three minutes what many a novelist has failed to do in volumes." Cirque du Soleil adapted this effect with the added use of strobe lights.

His skit "The 7 Deadly Sins" was one of his later creations, getting double mileage by portraying each sin in the form of its opposite.

He portrayed the characteristics of animals in "The Lion Tamer" and "Bip as a Bullfighter."

He mimed the elements, such as the wind.

He acted out vertigo in climbing a ladder. He dazzled the audience with his portrayal of trying to place a heavy piece of baggage

Backstage with Marcel
PHOTO: PEGGY HELLER

onto the overhead baggage rack on a jiggling train; he mimed sea sickness on a ship so effectively that we in the audience felt the tilt and the lurch of the swells. He performed "The Pickpocket," in which he used an all-black screen, spanning the width of the stage, to express the long arm attached to a thieving hand.

Marcel's study of the human condition—of the forces with which we struggle, the weight of emotion as carried in the soul, the conflicts that pull in all directions—was vast and complete. He gave the performance of a lifetime.

His audience, which included Hollywood's greats who knew well the difficulties and caprices of a career spanning over sixty years in the entertainment world, returned its appreciation of him with a twenty-minute standing ovation. It was a fitting historical moment in time.

He received me backstage for a brief visit. He looked very frail. The enormous energy with which he had just filled the theater for close to two hours was now drained. He was emptied of all but his essence. An image came to my mind of a filigreed leaf in which all the green had been worn away, except for the connecting network of veins.

He expressed regret that we couldn't have more time together, but said that he gave all his energy to his performances these days and had nothing left after the show.

Of course, having seen the show, I fully understood, and I savored one last electric jolt as we embraced for the last time.

For the next three years, Marcel continued to tour, though he cut back his performances from three hundred to one hundred fifty a year. His bookings were no longer what they used to be. Times had changed. He was no longer cutting the same figure on stage as he had in his prime. He had lost a lot of weight, and his memory was failing him. His hearing was more bad than good. His lifeline of performance and applause was fading into silence.

The money was gone. His mime school was forced to shut down for lack of funding. The school was his legacy, his link to the next generation of mimes. It must have been the blow that broke him.

I did a painted portrait of him from this last stage in his life. It depicts the finality of being done with his work on this earth, beseeching return to the Source.

The Supplication. Take me. I'm done.
PAINTING: PAULETTE FRANKL

80th Birthday | 159

I kept the cape and the lace top I'd worn on that first trip to Chicago for decades, but never used them again. Moths and silverfish ate away at the cape. I ended up selling it at the flea market for a costume. The delicate lace top I gave away to my oldest grandson's first girlfriend with a brief story of its inception. I told her I was giving her this gift that meant so much to me, because their love for each other was so pure.

Chapter 25
Homage

And so I hung up the phone that had jarred me awake in the early dawn in my casita in Santa Fe with the news of Marcel's passing. All day, I walked around in a daze as though the weave of our togetherness was coming unstrung.

News of Marcel's death was all over the media. A saddened world responded by honoring this graceful ambassador of unity, humor, and grace with two minutes of silence, his signature, his legacy. It was fitting that upon his death, the entire world paid him tribute with two minutes of hushed appreciation.

Then came the talking heads and the analyses. It was strange and difficult to hear his life and accomplishments reduced to sound bites.

Had I been given the opportunity to write his obituary, this is what I would have said:

> *The world's greatest mime, Marcel Marceau, and his alter ego Bip, died on Saturday night, September 22, 2007, on the holiest of Jewish holidays. Yom Kippur is the day that frees the body and regenerates the soul. Was it divine intervention that determined the propitious date of departure from the earthly plane, or was it another example of his perfect timing?*
>
> *His life was much more than being the world's greatest mime, or that he had studied under the great masters Charles Dullin and Etienne Decroux and performed with Jean-Louis Barrault, or that he took mime out of the streets and into the greatest theaters in the world, or that he was a war hero who saved countless Jewish children from the certain death at the hands of the Gestapo, or that he had*

fought alongside the Yankees in General George Patton's battalion, or that he was an artist and printmaker par excellence, or that he had won awards as Ambassador for Peace and Aging.

Beneath his illustrious whiteface stage persona was a man struggling with the battles of ego and insecurity, talents and failures, great strengths and great weaknesses. He was at once both dominant and submissive in his constant struggle with these aspects of himself. The whipmaster was always on his back, always pushing him to his limits, never satisfied, always demanding more. This man of a thousand personas was pulled in multiple directions, blessed with the glories of success, and enslaved with the need to uphold his image as a world icon in spite of changing times and a diminishing audience.

Onstage, his message was about the bravados, frailties, and foibles of the human condition. It was a testimony that people the world over of any age shared a common bond of understanding, not through their diverse languages but through the recognition of their common emotions. Offstage, it was about the pain of loss, the joy of fleeting moments, the insatiable need for approval, and the complex and messy matters of the heart.

Onstage, he turned silence into a universal language. Offstage, he used silence as a shield to protect and disguise his vulnerability.

Onstage, he made the invisible visible. Offstage, he made the visible tangibly invisible!

As a performing artist he was unparalleled, without equal. Bip was his symbol of everyman, the rugged survivor of all that life dished out. Bip was the receptacle of Marcel's emotions, all that he wouldn't own, once removed. Marcel, the man, suffered life's blows the same as anyone, only larger.

Marcel and Bip toured the world nonstop for more than fifty years, performing on stages in at least one hundred fifty countries, three hundred nights a year to express, above all, the universal understanding of love, fear, humor, compassion, and hope eternal to people of all ages. His life was his stage and his art form.

Both Marcel Marceau and Bip carved out their niche of immortality in history. Marcel, the man, died at age eighty-four; his alter ego Bip was sixty. Marceau left behind two sons, two daughters, and three ex-wives. Bip left behind a world-following of orphaned students and devotees. Neither left any successor to the throne.

I had the good fortune to know both Marceau and Bip—intimately.

Samuel Avital, Founder and Director of Le Centre du Silence Mime School in Boulder, Colorado, and Marcel had a complex and sometimes stormy relationship. One example seems to sum it up: Marcel's chosen title for an autobiography (that he never completed) was My Silent Outcry. The title of Samuel Avital's autobiography, which he did complete, was Mime, The Silent Outcry: The Life and Times of Samuel Avital. Avital actually asked Marcel to write the introduction!

But Avital penned a moving eulogy of his own to Marcel in which he wrote, in part, "As far as I remember, I never had any conversation with Marceau on mundane matters or gossip, only lofty, meaningful, and practical subjects. He was a living question mark, probing and exploring the deeper dimensions of being, and how to express that with our beautiful art of silence—mime. He was a great silent lighthouse."

The President of France, Nicolas Sarkozy, said in a statement, "France loses one of its most eminent ambassadors." Prime Minister Francois Fillon praised Marcel as "the master" who possessed the rare gift of "being able to communicate with each and every one beyond the barriers of language."

A cartoon in The New Yorker depicted the Great Wall of France as a long line-up of mimes, *ad inifinitum,* mimicking Marcel's hand movements of a wall.

The Angel that had been cast down to Earth amidst the tumult of the tempest long ago was now called back home. His job was done. His time on Earth was complete.

Although I have been unable to determine the exact cause of his death, I venture to guess that his seemingly invincible health and energy could not withstand the receding tide of his life. The gravity of his problems finally outweighed the buoyancy of his energy. Since he was never one to miss a performance, he had to be physically removed, as if by a pratfall, by the hand of his Creator.

Some accounts say he died in a small hotel or pension in Cahors, France, with his daughter, Aurelia, at his side. Other accounts have him at the racetrack in Cahors, at the moment of death. I like to think that he "lived the death" with his eyes open, as he had so often instructed his students. I like to think that he watched, a one-man audience to his life being played out before him, and that he accepted it with a deep and poignant satisfaction. And I imagine that when the precise moment summoned him, he exited his body with grace and humility, to join forces in his wedding with eternity.

Where there's death, there are vultures.

Marcel died with $450,000 of debt that France extracted from him by auctioning off every single item of his life, including, probably, my letters to him. France made a monetary profit off the deal, but it was their loss. They destroyed the great work of art that was Marcel's earthly paradise and legacy: his Bercheres, home of all that he held sacred.

The vultures should have turned his magical farm house and ten-acre kingdom in Bercheres into a museum-shrine for tourists and anyone troubled by this troubled world in need of peace and restorative beauty, and the remembrance that life is simple unity, not war, power, and greed. The money France got from the auction was a drop in France's ocean of money, but they lost the haven-legacy that Marcel had built over his long, creative lifetime. It's heartbreaking. At least they waited till after his death to pull his life apart limb by limb, item by item.

Pere Lachaise Cemetery occupies 110 acres in the 20th arrondissement of Paris and dates back to 1804. It's the largest cemetery in Paris, with more than a million bodies buried there. It's believed to be the most visited cemetery in the world, with hundreds of thousands of people stopping there every year. It also might be said that it's one of the few democratic places of its kind, hosting the remains of commoners and many of the most influential people in world history and certainly the history of France, including Abelard and Eloise, Apollinaire, Balzac, Chopin, Colette, Maria Callas, Daumier, Delacroix, Isadora Duncan, Jim Morrison, and Marcel Marceau.

One of the great rabbis of France, Rene-Samuel Sirat, presided over the ceremony of Marcel's memorial service. At his burial ceremony, the second movement of Mozart's Piano Concerto No. 21 was played; Marcel performed his "Creation of the World" to this music. Also played was the Sarabande of Bach's Cello Suite No. 5. Fall leaves fluttered gently to the ground.

    Although notice of his memorial service did not reach many of those close to him, myself included, some three hundred people were present. It was posted online that another billion watched it on TV. Marcel's Medals of Honor were placed on a red satin pillow on the foot of the coffin. Bip's burlap opera hat appeared on a stand of its own at the head of the coffin. The body of Marcel was interred in a simple grave about the size of a phone booth, but Bip's top hat managed to escape burial. Bip lives on!

    A short distance away, a young man dressed in white tennis shoes, white pants, white shirt, and the large white feathered wings of an angel stood in a posture typical of Marcel. I like to imagine that this angel was thinking of the eloquence, goodness, and strength that Marcel brought to this world in his lifetime. He never quit; he kept on performing until shortly before his death at age eighty-four. I like to think that this angel was waiting to spirit him away.

People wrote comments in a guest book that was posted online. One message that caught my eye was from Liz Peryam Reshower of Pisgah Forest, North Carolina, that read "Finally got out of that box, did you?"

A beautiful message by Arne Folkedal read, "He held the final pose as the stage light extinguished to black. In the blackout which remained for nearly a minute, there was a palpable silence in the house. No one shifted in a seat. No one coughed or whispered or made any sound at all. Each of us had been touched to our innermost, seldom-reached essence. Nothing need be said, so there was complete, absolute silence."

Portrait of Marcel Marceau
PAINTING:
PAULETTE FRANKL
PHOTO REFERENCE:
LE MIME MARCEL MARCEAU ENTRTIENS ET REGARDS
BY VALERIE BOCHENEK

CHAPTER 26

Beyond Mime, Beyond Time

"Come to the edge!" the voices called. "We can watch the storm that's happening!" Everyone rushed forward, ahead. All but one. No sooner had I squared my stance on the deck of the rolling ship to behold the storm at sea when a thin hand, an otherworldly hand, closed itself around my own and pulled me back inside.

"Here is where it's happening," said the presence. "It's all happening here, inside."

The presence showed me some of its magnificent otherworldly art. And I knew then that I, too, was meant to create and produce art that expressed itself from the inside.

Waking up from the dream, I also realized that my trip to France, to Marcel's grave, was not so much about seeing what was happening *there*, in Bercheres and Paris and at Cimetiere du Pere Lachaise, as what was happening in *here*, in the embrace of my perception.

For now, it was enough to know that Marcel and I had another date: March 22, 1985, on what would have been his eighty-fifth birthday.

So I made the pilgrimage to France and his grave site the following spring.

First stop was his house in Bercheres, in the Loire region of Normandy, approximately an hour's drive from Paris. My dear friend Bruno Walerski met me at Charles de Gaulle Airport and away we went, from my house to Marcel's house, so to speak, with only the long flight, passport control, and Paris traffic in between. We lunched at the local restaurant, then walked toward Marcel's property in the direction indicated by the owner/chef. When we asked for more specific directions from a passing driver, she waved her arm in a large arc.

"What does that mean?" I queried.

"All of it," she replied. "This entire block is his property."

He had a ten-acre estate in the residential center of town, with hills and a small forest. We came to a high double wooden gate that was locked, midway along the tall ivy-covered fence. We pressed our faces against the keyhole of the gate in an attempt to see inside. We caught a glimpse of his blooming garden, a sliver of his three-hundred-year-old farmhouse, and a number of the three thousand trees he'd planted and nurtured. I strained to see his atelier, constructed in the same style as the farmhouse, where he painted, wrote, and perfected his pantomimes in front of a long practice mirror. This was as close as I ever got to visiting Marcel at his home. But pressing forward while being shut out became the metaphor of my pilgrimage to find Marcel.

Back in Paris, we braved the morning commute on the Metro to see the theater where he first performed and his school of mime, now closed. We bucked rain, hail, snow, and wind to visit the Bibliotheque Nationale de Paris, waiting for hours to have dossiers drawn up in order to request and view videos of him. The library closed before we saw much of anything, but the material I sought was there and it was apparent that I needed much more time, probably weeks, to sort through it all.

Our last stop was the Cimetiere du Pere Lachaise. I found it to be a lively place, beautifully situated on a hillside overlooking Paris, with winding walkways and old-growth trees arching over the graves. However, I was shocked at the degree of disrepair that many of the sites suffered, and how crowded it was, both with the living and the dead. Sculptures of and by famous people are missing noses, fingers, and penises from vandalism.

But above all, the energy in this cemetery is stimulating and, dare I say, sexy! Great genius is high-energy; a high level of libido goes with the territory. The body may no longer be alive, but the energy remains. For example, when Jim Morrison was first interred, it was necessary to keep a twenty-four-hour guard on his gravesite, because people snuck in at night to have sex on his grave.

We arrived at last at Marcel's gravesite in the rain. His grave was smaller than I'd expected. Old dead flowers evidenced that others had visited the site. I expected it to be more adorned with fresh blooms on his eighty-fifth birthday, more like Chopin or Jim Morrison's graves. We seemed to be the only people there expressly for *him*. My bouquets of spring tulips, daffodils, and pink roses for this March 22, the day of his birth and the day after the equinox, were the only fresh offering of flowers at that time.

Standing there at Marcel's small gravesite, looking at the dead flowers and his unflattering photo in a plastic sleeve, with Bip's hat long gone, I recalled the rumor that his immediate family wanted nothing to do with his fans; they were closed to everyone and had even said that now that he was dead, mime was dead along with him. I felt utterly viscerated. I communed with the emptiness.

And there, in the emptiness, in the silence, yet again, was Marcel, reminding me that the weight of our human burden becomes lighter the deeper we dare to go, and therein lies the secret and the source of all things. Deepen the search and ye shall find.

Sketch for Paulette by Marcel Marceau, 1972

It was an end, but like everything in duality, it was also a beginning. I knew I could now finally fathom the wisdom of this great man, this unlikely gentle prophet in the guise of a hapless Bip. While he was alive, I was too caught up in my own projections, desires, and entanglements of should, would, and could. I was lost in illusion. In my search for the man who was a god onstage, I didn't realize I was being touched by an angel with a broken wing.

The Marcel I loved was not buried in a box in this hole in the ground, covered with plastic AstroTurf and a few flowers. The Bip I loved wasn't represented here at all. No.

Instead, they were both alive and well in my heart. They brought me to this place to show me that, though life doesn't survive death, love and illusion definitely do!

I suddenly experienced a ferocious hunger, not only for life, but for lunch!

Postscript

In spring 2013, I traveled to California in search of Marcel's courtship letters to include in this book.

I turned my storage locker upside down. I removed everything. I carefully went through every box and trunk to find the missing letters. They just *had* to be somewhere!

The door to the locker was propped open and my entire life was laid out on the blacktop: journals, photos, memorabilia, costumes, artwork, but not those special letters from Marcel which I placed somewhere for the safekeeping. Crestfallen, I packed to return to Santa Fe, empty-handed.

The day before I was scheduled to leave, I received an email about a fundraising dinner the following week at the Museum of the Performing Arts in San Francisco, honoring Marcel Marceau's love letters to a longtime lover, a mime in the Bay Area. The event was titled, "Marcel Marceau: A Love Affair."

A gift from the gods! The magnificence of manifestation!

Surely, I was that lover! How many Bay Area mimes could he have had way back then?

This was my chance to get copies of those missing letters and celebrate the dinner. Perfect timing! I could even read excerpts from the book.

I spent the day feverishly trying to contact someone on the committee of the event for verification.

Finally, at the eleventh hour, I received an email from the event planner. "Thank you very much, but you are *not* The One, and it would be inappropriate for you to attend the dinner."

Ahhhhhh! The enduring power of illusion!

About the Author

Paulette Frankl

In *Marcel & Me,* Paulette Frankl calls to the fore all her life experiences as artist, story teller, wordsmith, mime, magician, musician, farmer, and sensualist to bring to life the magical wonderment of Marcel Marceau. The reader accompanies her as she gets to know the greatest mime of all time onstage and off, as a friend, lover and a legacy.

Paulette's first public art exhibit was at the age of seven for the sophisticated Los Angeles art world in a joint show with her father, Austrian-born world-renowned Art Deco furniture designer, Paul T. Frankl.

As a photo-journalist in Europe, she was a staff photographer for Gruner & Jahr. Her publication credits include Twen, Eltern and a cover and lead article on the hippie movement in California for France's *Réalités.* The magazine *Geo* profiled her lifestyle in California in the seventies.

As a performance artist in the field of mime and magic, she was featured on Italian television at Carnival in Venice, and appeared in *Sunset Magazine.* She worked as a professional magician in Las Vegas, Nevada, the magic capital of the world. Her creative association with Marcel Marceau as friend, muse, and lover spanned thirty-six years.

Her courtroom art has been aired on CNN, NBC, ABC, CBS, FOX, WGN-TV and "Talk America," and has taken her all the way to the United States Supreme Court.

Frankl's fine art combines the visual with the visceral to engender a live force in an original style she calls Perceptualism. Her art was on exhibit at a group show titled *XV Santa Fe Artists* at the Las Vegas Art Museum in 2005.

Ms. Frankl is a graduate of Stanford University; she holds a BA in art and languages. Born into a world of art and aesthetics, her formal study in art included a one-month summer camp at the Skowhegan School of Painting and Sculpture in Skowhegan, Maine, where her work won honorable mention for originality.

Frankl is a painter with words as well as with pen and brush. Her first book, *Lust for Justice, The Radical Life and Law of J. Tony Serra* has been on Amazon's digital bestseller list in its category for more than three years.

Paulette resides in Santa Fe, New Mexico where she shares her life with a mystical cat and ravens and many beloved friends.

Printed in Great Britain
by Amazon